所有选文均来自腾讯网《中国人的一天》栏目

中国人的生活故事
（第二辑）七十古稀

Stories of Chinese People's Lives II
People in Their 70s

孔子学院总部/国家汉办 编

外语教学与研究出版社
FOREIGN LANGUAGE TEACHING AND RESEARCH PRESS
北京 BEIJING

图书在版编目 (CIP) 数据

中国人的生活故事. 第二辑. 七十古稀 / 孔子学院总部/国家汉办编. —— 北京：外语教学与研究出版社，2016.9
ISBN 978-7-5135-8141-7

Ⅰ. ①中… Ⅱ. ①孔… Ⅲ. ①汉语－阅读教学－对外汉语教学－自学参考资料 Ⅳ. ①H195.4

中国版本图书馆 CIP 数据核字 (2016) 第 235017 号

出 版 人	蔡剑峰
项目策划	郑丽慧　李 丹
责任编辑	向凤菲
执行编辑	郑丽慧
英文编辑	张立萍
装帧设计	姚 军
出版发行	外语教学与研究出版社
社　　址	北京市西三环北路 19 号（100089）
网　　址	http://www.fltrp.com
印　　刷	北京盛通印刷股份有限公司
开　　本	787×1092　1/24
印　　张	7.5
版　　次	2016 年 10 月第 1 版 2016 年 10 月第 1 次印刷
书　　号	ISBN 978-7-5135-8141-7
定　　价	49.00 元

购书咨询：（010）88819926　电子邮箱：club@fltrp.com
外研书店：https://waiyants.tmall.com
凡印刷、装订质量问题，请联系我社印制部
联系电话：（010）61207896　电子邮箱：zhijian@fltrp.com
凡侵权、盗版书籍线索，请联系我社法律事务部
举报电话：（010）88817519　电子邮箱：banquan@fltrp.com
法律顾问：立方律师事务所　刘旭东律师
　　　　　中咨律师事务所　殷　斌律师
物料号：281410001

"中国人的生活故事（第二辑）"
编辑委员会

总策划：许　琳

总监制：夏建辉　蔡剑峰

监　制：苗　强

编写委员会成员（姓名按音序排列）：

樊克亚　郝　文　李　丹

陆筱俊　苗　强　杨　益

袁　玥　郑丽慧

翻译（姓名按音序排列）：

陈　蕾　陈晓宇　胡　朦

彭　瑶　王琪瑜　于　欢

朱慧敏

出版说明

为满足海内外汉语学习者对汉语读物的需求,促进中外文化交流与了解,孔子学院总部/国家汉办继2015年策划、出版了《中国人的生活故事》(第一辑)之后,又启动了《中国人的生活故事》(第二辑)的编写、出版项目。

《中国人的生活故事》(第二辑)旨在通过讲述各行各业的普通中国人的一天,向各国汉语学习者展现平凡、真实又温暖人心的当代中国人的生活,介绍历史悠久又与时俱进的中国传统文化。

本系列读物共有7个分册,分别为:《弱冠桃李》《三十而立》《四十不惑》《五十知命》《六十花甲》《七十古稀》《耄耋之年》,呈现了从二十岁左右的年轻人到八九十岁的耄耋老人的生活状态和精神风貌。

本系列读物主要具有以下特色:

1. 选文内容真实、语言地道。每个分册收录6篇选文,均取材于腾讯网《中国人的一天》栏目,讲述6个民族、地区、职业等各不相同的人物的故事,以满足不同读者群体的阅读需求。

2. 每篇选文标注对应的HSK等级。根据生词、句长、文化点等的不同,将选文难度标为HSK4级到HSK6级不等,为不同汉语水平的读者提供参考。

3. 生词选择以《HSK考试大纲》中的"词汇大纲"为依据。选文生词以超纲词、HSK6级词、HSK5级词为主,重点难点词筛选后随文附注,提供相应的词性与英文释义。书后附有全书生词索引，方便读者查阅。

4.注重中国传统文化与当代中国风貌的呈现。文中具有文化特色的词语和网络流行用语随文单独列出，提供详细的中英文解释说明；每篇选文后设置"延伸阅读"板块，以中英文对照阅读的形式向读者进一步介绍与主题相关的文化事物和现象。

5.全书图文并茂，可读性强。选文正文配有相应的真实摄影照片，文化词汇的解释以及"延伸阅读"等板块也视需要提供配图，帮助读者更直观、形象地理解相应的文字说明。

6.注重阅读的趣味性和互动性。每篇选文后设置"文化链接"板块，读者通过扫描二维码可以获得与选文主题相关的图片、音频、视频、网站等丰富的在线资源。另外，还有设计旗袍等趣味性活动配合阅读主题。

《中国人的生活故事》（第二辑）系列读物精读、泛读皆宜，既可用于辅助教师课堂教学，也适合学习者课外阅读学习。希望本系列读物可以为海内外的汉语学习者打开一扇了解当代中国之窗，也希望读者通过阅读本系列图书加深对中国经济、社会、民俗、地理的了解，学习到全新、鲜活、实用的汉语。

外语教学与研究出版社
2016年9月

Publisher's Note

To satisfy the demand for reading materials for Chinese learners at home and abroad and to promote intercultural communication and understanding, the Confucius Institute Headquarters (Hanban) has commissioned the compilation and publication of the second series of *Stories of Chinese People's Lives*, after the publication of its first series in 2015.

Through descriptions of an ordinary day for Chinese people from all walks of life, the second series of *Stories of Chinese People's Lives* aims to share real and heartwarming life stories from contemporary Chinese people and to introduce the ancient and yet constantly evolving Chinese culture to Chinese learners worldwide.

This series contains seven books: *People in Their 20s*, *People in Their 30s*, *People in Their 40s*, *People in Their 50s*, *People in Their 60s*, *People in Their 70s*, and *People in Their 80s and 90s*. These books serve to illustrate the daily lives and outlooks of people of all ages.

The second series of *Stories of Chinese People's Lives* has the following features:

1. Texts in each book are true stories written in authentic Chinese. Each book includes six texts, all of which are drawn from the *One Day, One Life* column on QQ.com. To satisfy the interests of different and diverse groups of readers, each book tells the stories of six people from various ethnic groups, regions and professions.

2. Each text corresponds to a specific HSK level. Based on its vocabulary, sentence length and cultural elements, each text is marked between HSK 4 and HSK 6 as a reference for learners at different levels.

3. The key words in each text are selected based on the vocabulary syllabus in the *HSK Test Syllabus*, and are mainly composed of words at or above HSK 5 and HSK 6. These key words are listed alongside the text and parts of speech and

definitions are explained in English. A glossary is attached at the end of each book for the readers' reference.

4. The presentation of both traditional and contemporary Chinese culture is equally stressed. Words containing cultural elements and Internet buzzwords are highlighted and illustrated alongside the text with detailed annotations in both Chinese and English. Each text is followed by a reading section called Extensive Reading, which contains a further bilingual introduction of related cultural events or phenomena.

5. Each book is made very readable with attractive pictures and well-written texts. Real life photos are correspondingly arranged on every page of the texts. The words containing cultural elements and the Extended Reading passages are also complimented with pictures to make them more visually engaging.

6. The books stress an amusing and interactive reading experience. A Cultural Links section is set in each text, which allows readers to scan QR codes to gain access to a wealth of online resources, including related images, audio files, videos and websites. In addition, there are interesting activities attached (such as designing a mandarin gown) to correspond with themes of the texts.

The second series of *Stories of Chinese People's Lives* is applicable to both intensive and extensive reading. The books can be used as classroom materials for teachers and also as extra-curricular reading materials for Chinese learners. We hope that this series of books will open a window for Chinese learners, both at home and abroad, to learn more about contemporary China. We also hope that reading these books will help learners to deepen their understanding of China's economy, society, traditional customs, and geography; as well gain a modern, fresh and useful Chinese vocabulary.

Foreign Language Teaching and Research Press
September, 2016

生词词性缩略形式表

英文缩写	英文全称	中文名称
n.	noun	名词
p.n.	proper noun	专有名词
v.	verb	动词
adj.	adjective	形容词
num.	numeral	数词
m.	measure word	量词
pron.	pronoun	代词
adv.	adverb	副词
prep.	preposition	介词
conj.	conjunction	连词
part.	particle	助词
int.	interjection	叹词
ono.	onomatopoeic word	拟声词

目录 CONTENTS

"猫咪控"
A Cat Lover

八年如一日,周大爷为无家可归的猫咪们建起了一个个温暖的家。

For the past eight years, Grandpa Zhou has built many warm homes for stray cats.

明星老人
An Elderly Star

70 岁的田春生坚持每天去公园锻炼身体,还出演过很多电影和电视连续剧。

The 70-year-old Tian Chunsheng exercises every day in the park. He has played roles in many films and TV serials.

外婆的千层底
Grandma's Multi-layer Outsoles

76 岁的外婆做了一辈子的千层底布鞋。

My 76-year-old grandma has made cloth shoes with multi-layer outsoles for her entire lifetime.

七旬老票友
A 75-year-old Amateur Beijing Opera Performer

正月里的焦家"大趴"
The Big Party at the Jiaos' in the First Lunar Month

古城"老顽童"
The "Kidult" in an Ancient Town

七旬老人追梦京剧，小角色也有大乐趣。

一年一度的大团圆展现的是一个四世同堂大家庭的幸福生活。

这是一个75岁高龄"老顽童"乐活晚年的故事。

A 75-year-old man pursues his dream of performing in Beijing opera, enjoying even the small roles.

The annual reunion shows the happy life of a four-generation family.

This is a story about a 75-year-old "kidult" enjoying his happy twilight years.

"Māomīkòng"
"猫咪控"
A Cat Lover

74岁的退休教师周大爷是个不折不扣的"猫咪控"。八年来,他坚持每天奔走喂养流浪猫,还记录下了他和小猫之间的点点滴滴。

Grandpa Zhou, a 74-year-old retired teacher, is truly a cat lover. He has fed stray cats every day for the past eight years, and recorded bits and pieces of his memories with them.

74岁的青岛退休教师周大爷是个不折不扣的"猫咪控"。八年来,他坚持每天奔走几公里喂养流浪猫,一天两顿饭,在五个喂养点之间来回奔波。他还给猫建立档案,为猫写了数百字的打油诗,以此记录他和小猫之间的点点滴滴。

> **~控 ~kòng**
> 网络用语,源于英文单词"complex"(情结)的前缀"com",指痴迷于某人或某物的人。
> *Kong* is an Internet buzzword that comes from the prefix "com" of the word "complex", referring to people who are obsessed with someone or something.

不折不扣	bùzhé-búkòu		downright; sheer
猫咪	māomī	n.	cat; kitty
喂养	wèiyǎng	v.	raise; keep
流浪	liúlàng	v.	roam about; drift around
奔波	bēnbō	v.	rush/dash about
档案	dàng'àn	n.	file; archive; record
点点滴滴	diǎndiǎndīdī		bit

● 打油诗 dǎyóushī

一种富有趣味性的诗体，相传这种诗体最早的作者叫张打油，所以叫"打油诗"。这类诗一般通俗易懂，诙谐幽默。

It is a kind of poem with amusing nature. It is said that its name comes from the writer of the first "dayou poem", Zhang Dayou. This kind of poem is usually easy to understand and humorous.

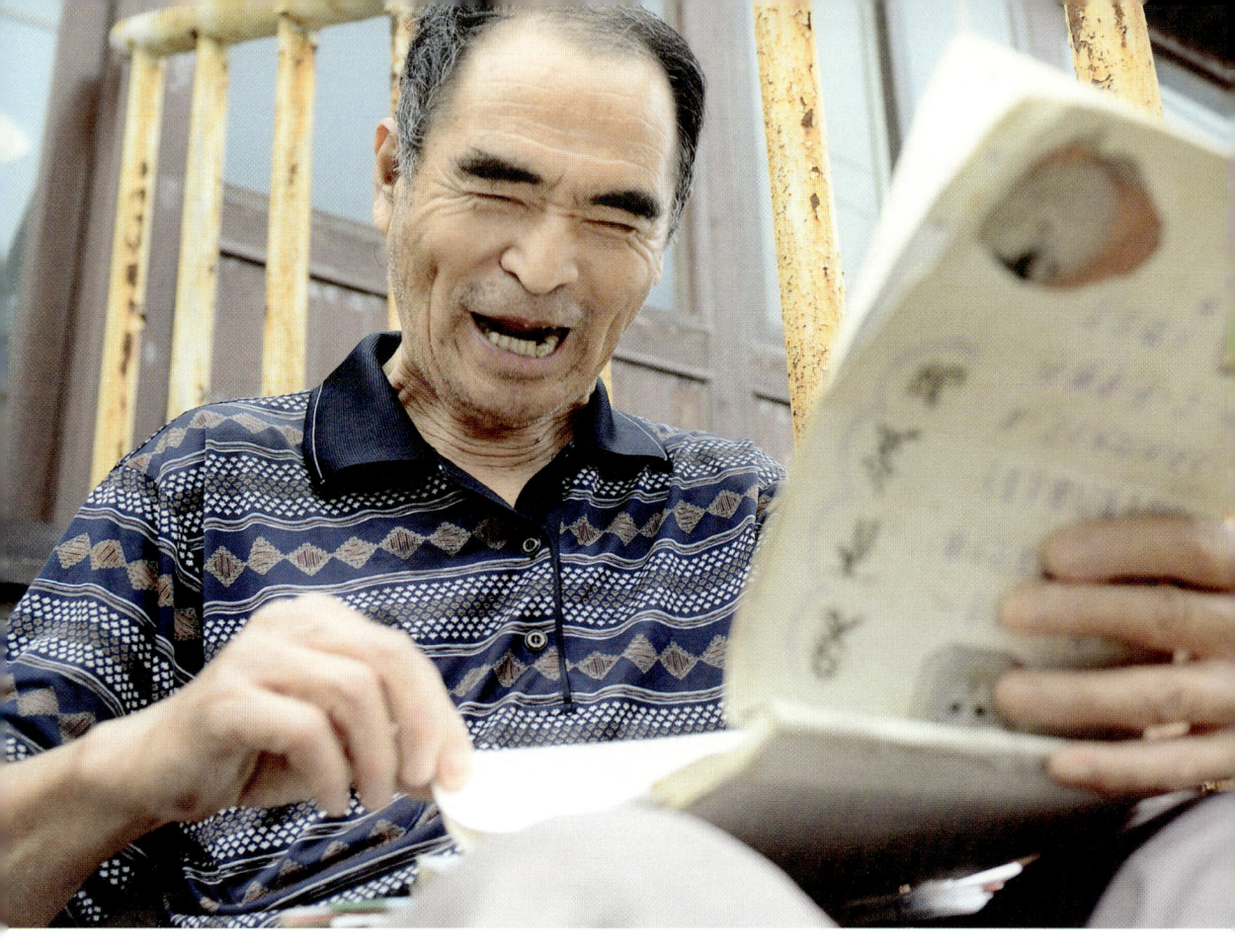

  周大爷从小就对猫咪情有独钟,退休后,养猫成了他生活中很重要的一部分。在他看来,猫是可爱的动物,流浪猫值得被关心、照料。

  八年前,由于老伴儿的身体原因,周大爷不得不把自己的几只爱猫送给别人。之后他便开始喂养社区周边的流浪猫。

情有独钟	qíngyǒudúzhōng		show special preference/favour to
照料	zhàoliào	v.	take care of; attend to
老伴儿	lǎobànr	n.	(of old couple) husband or wife
社区	shèqū	n.	community
周边	zhōubiān	n.	neighbouring area

语文老师出身的周大爷把猫咪的故事全都记在了本子上,并配上铅笔画和照片,可谓图文并茂。

出身	chūshēn	n.	one's previous experience or occupation
配	pèi	v.	match
可谓	kěwèi	v.	it may/can be called
图文并茂	túwén-bìngmào		(of a book, magazine, etc) be excellent in both pictures/illustrations and texts

记者跟着周大爷来喂猫，猫咪警觉地看着镜头。

警觉	jǐngjué	adj.	alert
镜头	jìngtóu	n.	camera lens
满脸	mǎnliǎn	n.	entire face
笑意	xiàoyì	n.	smile
栅栏	zhàlan	n.	railings; fence
对视	duìshì	v.	look at each other
善良	shànliáng	adj.	kind-hearted
主人	zhǔrén	n.	owner; possessor

每次来喂猫,周大爷都满脸笑意。

栅栏外的猫咪和周大爷对视。它和这位善良的"主人"已经非常熟悉。

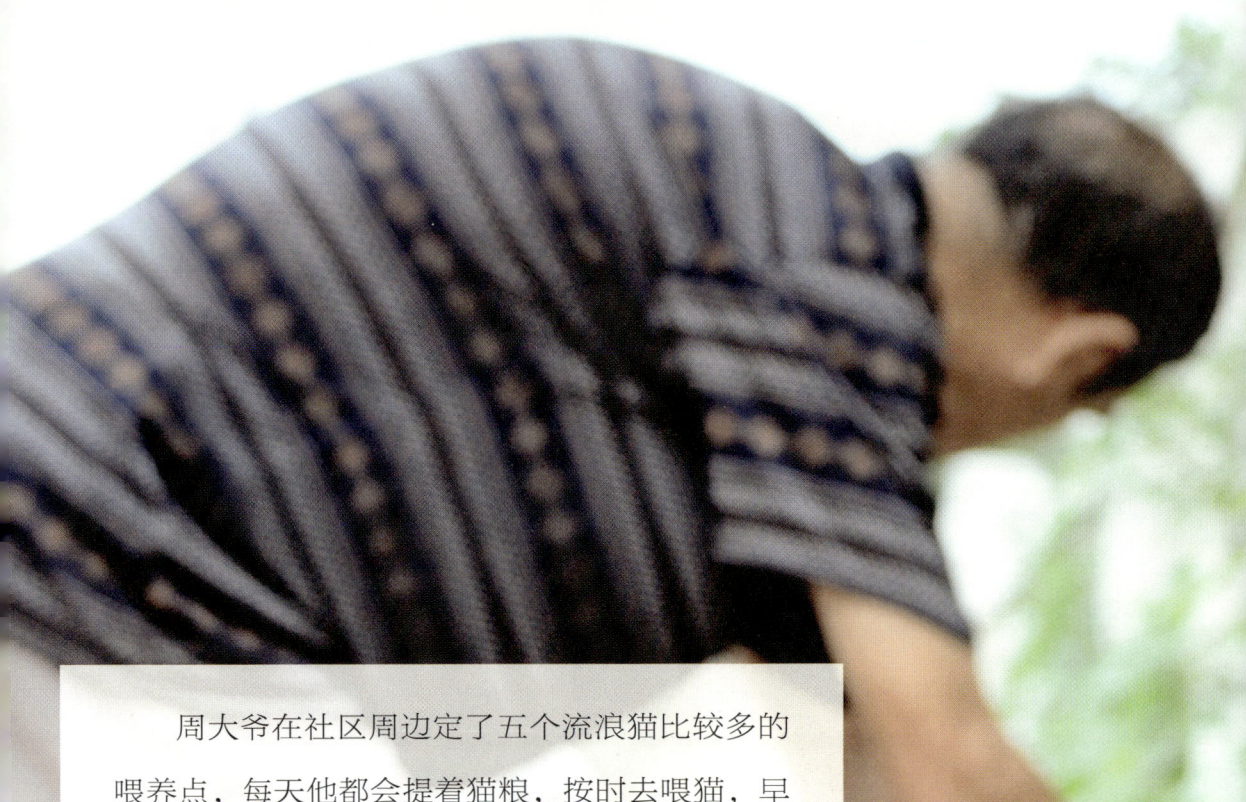

周大爷在社区周边定了五个流浪猫比较多的喂养点，每天他都会提着猫粮，按时去喂猫，早上五点一次，下午四点一次。八年如一日，风雨无阻。周大爷每个月要花500块钱购买猫粮。

风雨无阻	fēngyǔ-wúzǔ		stopped neither by wind nor rain—regardless of wind and rain
购买	gòumǎi	v.	buy; purchase
猫粮	māoliáng	n.	cat food

几年下来,他喂养的流浪猫数量从最初的几只变成了现在的34只。周大爷说:"期间也有猫去世了,或者走丢了,但数量还是越来越多。"

三狸花、飞毛腿、小白脸、大黄……周大爷给34只猫都起了名字,他对它们的性格和外形特点也都了如指掌。

期间	qījiān	n.	time; period
去世	qùshì	v.	die; pass away
外形	wàixíng	n.	appearance
了如指掌	liǎorúzhǐzhǎng		know sb/sth like the palm of one's hand—know thoroughly

周大爷只要在路上遇到流浪猫,就会把随身带着的食物散给它们。

灌到空矿泉水瓶里的水是周大爷给猫咪喝的。

随身	suíshēn	adj.	have/take/bring sth with oneself
散	sàn	v.	distribute; give out
灌	guàn	v.	fill; pour
矿泉水	kuàngquánshuǐ	n.	mineral water

一包猫粮，几瓶水，周大爷每天都要提着这些东西走上几公里。

谈及将来，周大爷说，他想继续记录他和流浪猫之间的故事。

（本文选编自 http://news.qq.com/original/oneday/1706.html，作者：孙志文。）

谈及	tánjí	v.	speak about

 Extensive Reading

中国的十二生肖
The Chinese Zodiac

十二生肖，也叫"十二属相"，是中国人传统上用来计算年龄的十二种动物，分别是鼠、牛、虎、兔、龙、蛇、马、羊、猴、鸡、狗、猪。在中国，每个人一出生就有一种动物做他的生肖，比如在农历猴年出生的人就属猴。

十二生肖在中国的传统文化中都有其独特的形象。

老鼠胆小多疑，人们常用"胆小如鼠"说一个人胆子小。牛主要用于农耕，所以中国人对牛的感情很深，认为牛勤劳、不求回报。勇猛威武的老虎则被人们认为是孩子的保护神，所以以前小孩子常戴虎头帽、穿虎头鞋。兔子在中国的传统故事中常常是聪明机智的角色,现在人们常用"动如脱兔"来形容一个人行动起来像飞跑的兔子一样敏捷。龙是人们用想象创造出来的,作为力量和精神的象征,龙一直备受中国人喜爱,"望子成龙"说的就是父母希望子女能有大成就,像龙一样高贵杰出。蛇多以负面形象出现,常被用来形容狠毒之人。马在中国人心中是忠诚、勤恳、有灵性的,人们用"马到成功"形容做事情很快就取得成功。羊一直被认为是温顺又善良的,"替罪羊"现在是指替别人受罪的人。猴子是机灵、调皮的,中国古典名著《西游记》中的孙悟空形象就是猴子的典型代表。另外,鸡的守时、狗的忠诚也是大家公认的,肥头大耳的猪则象征着福气。

你是不是很好奇,十二生肖中为什么没有猫呢?据说是因为中国古代没有猫,而十二生肖在猫传入中国以前就已经产生了。

虎头帽

虎头鞋

The Chinese zodiac, also called the "Twelve Zodiac", refers to the twelve animals that Chinese people traditionally used to calculate people's ages. They are the rat, ox, tiger, rabbit, dragon, snake, horse, sheep, monkey, rooster, dog and pig. In China, everyone is born in a year with an animal assigned to that year. For example, a person born in the Year of the Monkey would be a Monkey.

Each animal in the zodiac has its unique traits in traditional Chinese culture.

Rats are timid and suspicious, and people often use "as timid as a rat" to describe a timid man. Oxen are mainly used for farming, so Chinese people have deep feelings towards them, regarding them as industrious animals that do not ask for anything in return. Mighty and brave tigers were thought to be the patron of children, so in old times children often wore tiger hats and tiger-headed shoes. Rabbits are often clever characters in traditional Chinese stories. Now people often use "move as a rabbit" to describe a person who is as agile as a running rabbit. Dragons are imaginary creatures. As an icon of physical and spiritual strength, the dragon has always been much loved by Chinese people. "Hoping my son will become a dragon" expresses the wish of parents for their children to achieve a big success in life, and to be as outstanding as a dragon. Snakes often appear in negative images, and are often used to describe vicious people. Horses are regarded by the Chinese people as loyal, hardworking and intelligent, and people use "achieving success when the horse arrives" to describe an immediate victory. Sheep are considered gentle and kind, and "scapegoat" describes someone who is blamed for faults of others. Monkeys are clever and naughty. The Monkey King in the Chinese classic *Journey to the West* is a typical image of the monkey. In addition, punctuality of the rooster and loyalty of the dog are well-recognised. A chubby pig is a symbol of blessings.

You might be curious as to why there is no cat in the zodiac. It is said that there were no cats in ancient China. The Chinese zodiac had been created before cats were introduced to China.

 **Cultural Links**

电影《十二生肖》讲述了一段寻找中国圆明园十二生肖中失散的四个兽首的故事。请扫描下方二维码，观看这部电影。

The Film *CZ12* tells a story of retrieving four bronze heads of Chinese zodiac animals from the Old Summer Palace. Please scan the QR code below to watch the film.

Míngxīng lǎorén
明星老人
An Elderly Star

HSK 5级

70岁的田春生是山西省西海子公园的一位"明星老人",迄今已在50多部影视剧中担任过不同角色,他每天都会来公园进行一些有难度的锻炼项目。

The 70-year-old Tian Chunsheng is an elderly star of the Xihaizi Park of Shanxi Province. He has played various roles in over 50 films and TV serials so far. He comes to the park to train himself by doing some difficult exercises every day.

　　70岁的田春生是山西省西海子公园的一位"大明星"。每天早上七点，他都会赶到公园锻炼身体。田春生不仅双杠玩得好，还是一位货真价实的明星。

双杠	shuānggàng	n.	parallel bars
货真价实	huòzhēn-jiàshí		out-and-out

田春生13岁进入山西太原戏剧学校学习须生，后来主攻丑角表演，毕业后成为一名丑角演员。

时至今日，田春生已在50余部影视剧中担任不同角色，而真正让他出名的，是在电视剧《亮剑》中扮演主人公李云龙的丈人。

主攻	zhǔgōng	v.	specialise (in a subject)
时至今日	shízhì-jīnrì		even to this day
出名	chūmíng	v.	gain repute; be famous
亮剑	Liàng Jiàn	p.n.	name of a TV serial
主人公	zhǔréngōng	n.	leading character (in a novel, film, etc)
丈人	zhàngren	n.	wife's father

● 须生 xūshēng
中国戏剧角色名，也称老生。扮演中老年男子，一般要戴胡须。
It is a role in traditional Chinese operas, also known as *laosheng*. *Xusheng* is usually a middle-aged or elderly male with a false beard.

● 丑角 chǒujué
中国戏剧角色名，一般扮演比较滑稽的角色。
It is a role in traditional Chinese operas. *Chou* characters are generally amusing.

胡子	húzi	n.	beard; moustache
守孝	shǒuxiào	v.	observe a period of mourning for one's deceased parent
坚守	jiānshǒu	v.	stick to
渐渐	jiànjiàn	adv.	gradually
标志	biāozhì	n.	sign; mark
梳理	shūlǐ	v.	comb

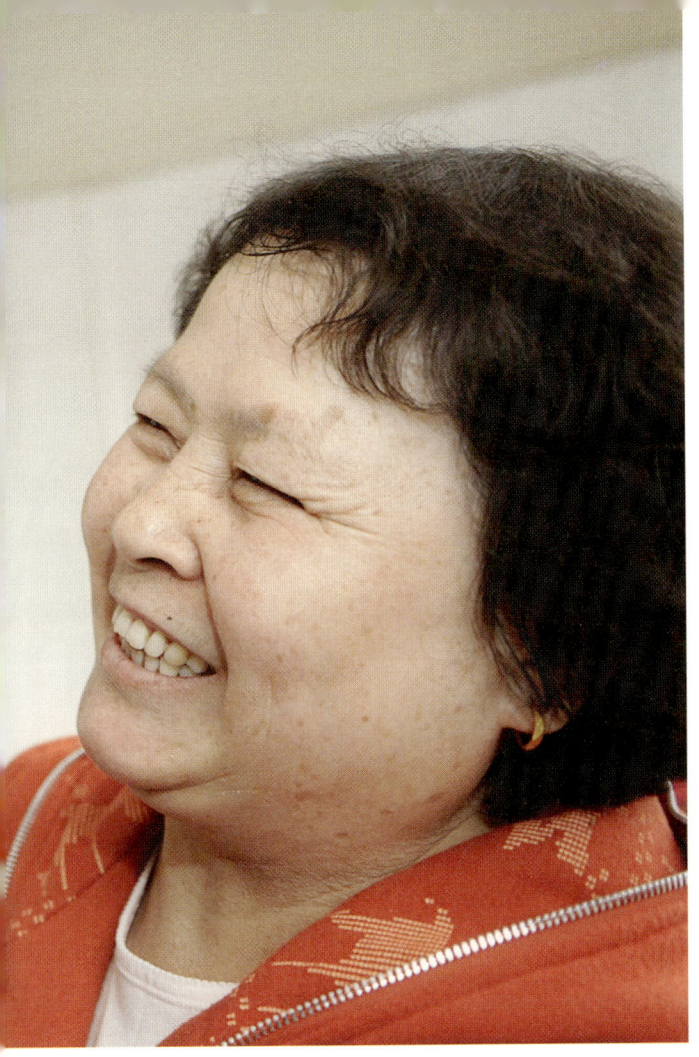

田春生的老伴儿在给他梳理胡子。

在田春生扮演的不同角色中，他那一把大胡子始终令人印象深刻。2000年，田春生的母亲去世，他为守孝而留起了胡子[1]。从那时起，田春生无论扮演什么角色，必坚守一个原则——宁可不演也不能剪胡子。他的胡子由短变长、由黑变白，也渐渐成为了他的标志。

---

1 中国古代习俗，现在已基本消失。

田春生不仅能演**文戏**，还能演**武戏**，甚至不用<u>替身</u>演员，这全<u>归功</u>于他的一<u>副</u>好<u>身板儿</u>。

> ● 文戏 wénxì
> 戏剧表演中以唱和演为主的戏。
> Gentle plays are plays that focus on singing and acting in traditional Chinese operas.
>
> ● 武戏 wǔxì
> 戏剧表演中以武打为主的戏。
> Martial plays are plays that focus on military acrobatics in traditional Chinese operas.

替身	tìshēn	n.	substitute; stand-in
归功	guīgōng	v.	give credit to
副	fù	m.	(for a set of things, etc)
身板儿	shēnbǎnr	n.	body; physique

在西海子公园，田春生每天都要完成一套自创的双杠动作。另外，举重、游泳、摔跤这些项目他也都很拿手。

每次田春生在双杠上游刃有余地做动作，都会让旁边的人既羡慕又佩服。

自创	zìchuàng	v.	create by oneself
举重	jǔzhòng	n.	weightlifting
摔跤	shuāijiāo	n.	wrestling
拿手	náshǒu	adj.	good/expert at
游刃有余	yóurèn-yǒuyú		handle a butcher's cleaver skillfully—do a job with skill and ease
羡慕	xiànmù	v.	admire; envy
佩服	pèifú	v.	admire; have admiration for

乐天派	lètiānpài	n.	optimist
性情	xìngqíng	n.	disposition; temperament
爽朗	shuǎnglǎng	adj.	hearty; frank and open
间隙	jiànxì	n.	gap; interval

田春生是个乐天派，他无论走到哪里都会给大家带去快乐。

性情爽朗的他爱交朋友，爱开玩笑，谁有什么不开心的事都会找他聊聊。

锻炼休息间隙，田春生会给大家讲笑话。

田春生还是个特别有情趣的人,闲暇时喜欢种种花草、养养鱼,还常常和一只养了多年的八哥对话。

情趣	qíngqù	n.	interest; taste
闲暇	xiánxiá	n.	leisure; free time
八哥	bāge	n.	mynah

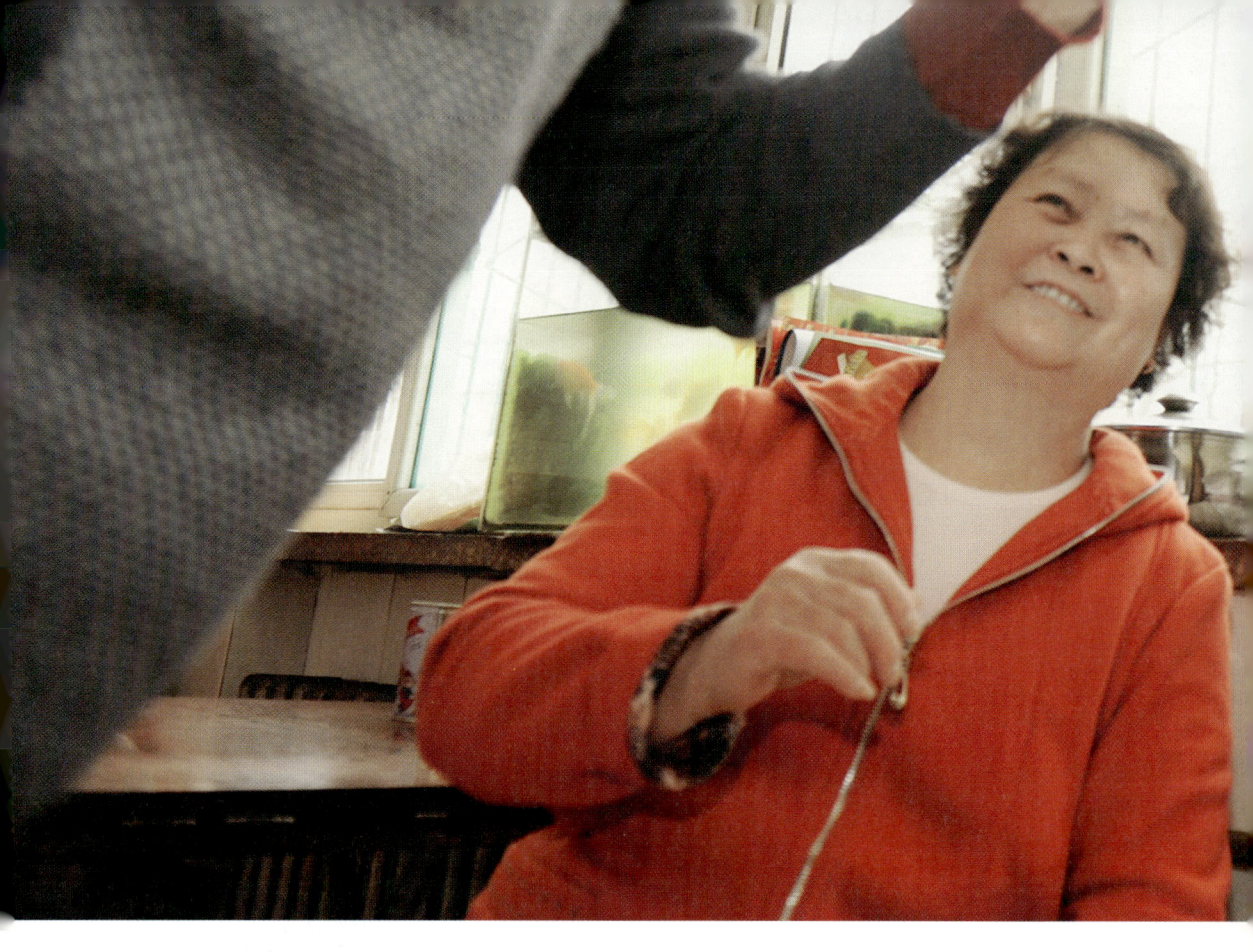

田春生的老伴儿是一名豫剧演员，常常陪着他练习台词。

| 豫剧 | yùjù | n. | Henan opera |
| 台词 | táicí | n. | actor's lines |

晚上看完《新闻联播》，田春生喜欢在书房上网，看看全球发生的新闻。在从心所欲之年，他依旧关心着天下之事。

（本文选编自 http://news.qq.com/original/oneday/1976.html，作者：寇宁。）

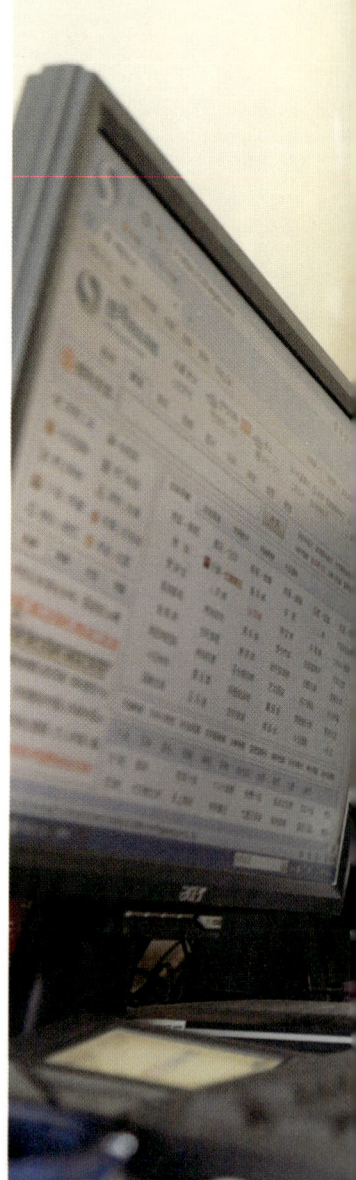

新闻联播	Xīnwén Liánbō	p.n.	name of a CCTV daily news programme
书房	shūfáng	n.	study
全球	quánqiú	n.	whole world; entire globe
从心所欲	cóngxīnsuǒyù		do as one pleases; follow one's inclinations
天下	tiānxià	n.	land under heaven—the world or the whole country

延伸阅读 Extensive Reading

公园里的"老有所乐"
Happiness for the Elderly in the Park

遛鸟

　　每天清晨，当大部分年轻人还在睡梦中时，北京很多公园里已经熙熙攘攘，随处可见老人们锻炼的身影了。

　　在晨练人群中，遛鸟的大爷们是起得最早的。他们提着鸟笼，四处转悠，时不时轻轻地把鸟笼前后摇晃着，这就是"遛鸟"。还有一些老人手拿扫帚般的大笔，蘸水在地上写字。这种不用纸墨，而是用水在地上进行书法练习的形式叫做"地书"。太极拳作为一种健身运动也深受老人们的喜爱。经常练习太极拳可以强身健体，锻炼身体的平衡感。老人们也喜欢在一起切磋棋艺，在公园坚持下棋20余年的唐大爷说："常下棋可以锻炼脑力，避免老年痴呆，你看我今年80岁了，可我从没感到自己老了。"公园里还有很多老年"乐队"，少则三五人，多则十几人。他们都是各种乐器的爱好者，在一起练习的时间久了，就组成了固定的"乐队"。公园既是天然练习场，也是实际上的表演舞台，每个"乐队"周围都有很多人围观欣赏。

　　近年来，这种在公园里兴起的"快乐文化"已经成为中国老年人修身养性的重要方式。老人们需要的不只是衣食饱暖，精神关爱也很重要。"我们也向往更丰富、更精彩的生活。小孩爱去游乐场，年轻人爱做运动，我们老人也需要'玩伴'。"一位老人这样说道。

Every morning, when the majority of young people are still asleep, many parks in Beijing are already bustling with the elderly doing exercise.

Amongst the morning crowd, the grandpas who walk their birds are the earliest. They walk around with a birdcage in their hands, tilting back and forth from time to time. This is called "walking birds". There are also some senior citizens writing on the ground by dipping water with a large broom-like brush. This is called "ground calligraphy", using no paper or ink but water to practise calligraphy on the ground. *Tai chi* as a body-building exercise is also much loved by the senior citizens. Regular practice of *tai chi* can help people keep fit and improve their sense of balance. Senior citizens also like to play Chinese chess together. Grandpa Tang, who has played Chinese chess in the park for over 20 years, said, "Regular practice of Chinese chess stimulates the brain and prevents Alzheimer's disease. You see, I am 80 years old, but I never feel old." There are also many senior "bands"

地书

in the park. One "band" consists of at least three to five people, or as many as a dozen people. They are lovers of various musical instruments who have been practising together for a long time, and eventually become a fixed "band". The park serves as a natural rehearsal place as well as an actual performance stage. Each "band" has a crowd of people surrounding and watching their performance.

In recent years, the rise of the "culture of happiness" in the park has become an important way of self-cultivation for the elderly in China. Senior citizens need more than just food and clothes; emotional support is also very important. "We aspire to a more colourful and exciting life. Children love to go to the playground, and young people love sports. We also need our 'playmates'," said one senior citizen.

太极拳

 Cultural Links

电影《飞越老人院》讲述了一群老人为了实现人生价值，寻找生命中纯粹的快乐与意义的故事。请扫描下方二维码，观看这部电影。

The film *Full Circle* tells a story of a bunch of senior citizens searching for pure joy and meaning in life to realise the value of their lives. Please scan the QR code below to watch the film.

HSK 5级

Wàipó de qiāncéngdǐ
外婆的千层底
Grandma's Multi-layer Outsoles

外婆从十来岁就开始学习纳鞋的手艺，今年76岁的她几十年如一日，一针一线地纳着千层底，已经亲手做了900多双布鞋了。

Grandma began to learn shoe-making craftsmanship when she was around 10 years old. Now at the age of 76, she has been making cloth shoes with multi-layer outsoles stitch by stitch for several decades, and has personally made over 900 pairs.

外婆生活在湖南省的一个小山村，和上世纪二三十年代出生的大多数土家族姑娘一样，今年76岁的外婆从十来岁时，就开始学习纳鞋。她从长辈手里传承了纳鞋手艺，几十年如一日，一针一线地纳着千层底。在她的印象中，自己做的布鞋有900多双了。

> ● 土家族 Tǔjiāzú
> 土家族是中国55个少数民族中的一个，主要居住在湖南、湖北、贵州、重庆等地区。织绣、剪纸、蜡染等是土家族的传统工艺。
>
> The Tujia ethnic group is one of China's 55 ethnic minorities, mainly dwelling in Hunan, Hubei and Guizhou provinces and Chongqing Municipality. Their traditional crafts include brocade and embroidery, paper-cutting, wax dyeing, etc.

山村	shāncūn	n.	mountain village
年代	niándài	n.	decade of a century
纳	nà	v.	sew close stitches (over)
传承	chuánchéng	v.	impart and inherit
针	zhēn	n.	needle
线	xiàn	n.	thread; string
千层底	qiāncéngdǐ	n.	multi-layer outsole
布鞋	bùxié	n.	cloth shoe

精致的小竹篓，放着针线、碎布、剪刀。"千层底"因其层数多而得名，尽管不是真的上千层，但每只鞋底起码也有二十多层。要将棉布用糨糊粘贴起来，晾干后剪成鞋样，中间放硬棕榈皮，然后一针一线地纳，一只鞋至少要用掉三根六米长的线。说起布鞋的故事和制作方法，外婆如数家珍。

竹篓	zhúlǒu	n.	bamboo basket/crate
碎布	suìbù	n.	cloth waste; rag
鞋底	xiédǐ	n.	sole
棉布	miánbù	n.	cotton (cloth)
糨糊	jiànghu	n.	paste
晾干	liànggān	v.	dry by airing
鞋样	xiéyàng	n.	shoe pattern
棕榈	zōnglǘ	n.	palm
如数家珍	rúshǔjiāzhēn		as if enumerating one's family treasures with pleasure— be very familiar with and proud of what one is talking about

"鞋底要一针一线地纳出来，做起来不容易，一天一个鞋底都做不完。"一大早，外婆取出鞋底，接着做前一天剩下的活儿。

在土家族的习俗里，嫁女儿或者娶媳妇时，给亲家的亲朋好友送一双布鞋，是必不可少的礼数。两年前，外婆还给我和妻子送了她亲手制作的布鞋作为新婚礼物，因为舍不得穿，我们一直珍藏着。

活儿	huór	n.	work; job
亲家	qìngjia	n.	relatives by marriage
亲朋好友	qīnpéng hǎoyǒu		one's relatives and close friends
必不可少	bìbùkěshǎo		essential; indispensable
礼数	lǐshù	n.	courtesy; etiquette
亲手	qīnshǒu	adv.	personally; with one's own hand
新婚	xīnhūn	v.	be newly married
珍藏	zhēncáng	v.	treasure

标注着尺码的鞋样是外婆用硬纸片剪成的。

按鞋样大小，将鞋底形状印在布上，剪下来，这是做鞋底的第一步。

外婆说，最初纳鞋底用麻线，麻线得自己搓，现在一般都用纱线。

鞋底厚度根据需要而重叠，做的时候要靠顶针、针夹子。

加一层布，修一次边，重叠十来层后，鞋底就基本做好了。

最后要把鞋底的毛边剪掉。

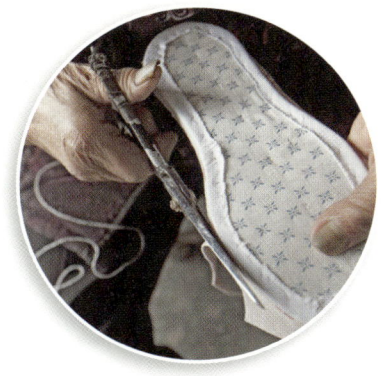

标注	biāozhù	v.	mark
尺码	chǐmǎ	n.	size
印	yìn	v.	print
麻线	máxiàn	n.	flaxen/linen thread
纱线	shāxiàn	n.	yarn
厚度	hòudù	n.	thickness
顶针	dǐngzhen	n.	thimble
毛边	máobiān	n.	(of cloth) rough selvage

不仅纳鞋底费事，做一个鞋帮也要经过十几道工序。一只鞋帮完全做好需要近三个半小时。

"趁身体好，多做几双。"外婆说。看着刚做好的布鞋，外婆满意地笑了。

费事	fèishì	v.	take a lot of trouble
鞋帮	xiébāng	n.	upper (of a shoe)
道	dào	m.	(for stages in a procedure)
工序	gōngxù	n.	working procedure; process

平时，村里年轻女人也来向外婆讨教做鞋的方法。如今，很多人追求怀旧和朴实的风格，手工布鞋透气、舒适，因此很受人们的青睐，不少人慕名上门来请外婆做鞋。

讨教	tǎojiào	v.	ask for advice; consult
怀旧	huáijiù	v.	be nostalgic
透气	tòuqì	v.	let in air
青睐	qīnglài	v.	show appreciation; bestow favour
慕名	mùmíng	v.	admire a famous person
上门	shàngmén	v.	drop in; visit

厚实的白底，素色的鞋帮，船样的外形，千层底布鞋的样子朴素而好看。

外婆说，做布鞋工序繁琐，慢工出细活。如今她年纪大了，手使不上力气，做起来更慢了，完全做好一双鞋子要花四五天时间。

素色	sùsè	n.	plain colour
朴素	pǔsù	adj.	(of colour, style, etc) simple; plain
繁琐	fánsuǒ	adj.	complicated and overloaded
慢工出细活	màngōng chū xìhuó		slow work yields fine products; soft fire makes sweet malt

细密的针脚,一针挨着一针排列,呈现小小的菱形,特别精致。做好的鞋上看不到一个线头。我知道,那层层叠叠、细细密密的针眼,是老人一辈子也割舍不下的情缘。平日里,一有空闲,她便做起鞋底来。"有人喜欢它,我就高兴。要是年轻人愿意拿起针线纳布鞋,不让这门手艺丢了,那就更好了!"

(本文选编自http://news.qq.com/original/oneday/1949.html,作者:周敏。)

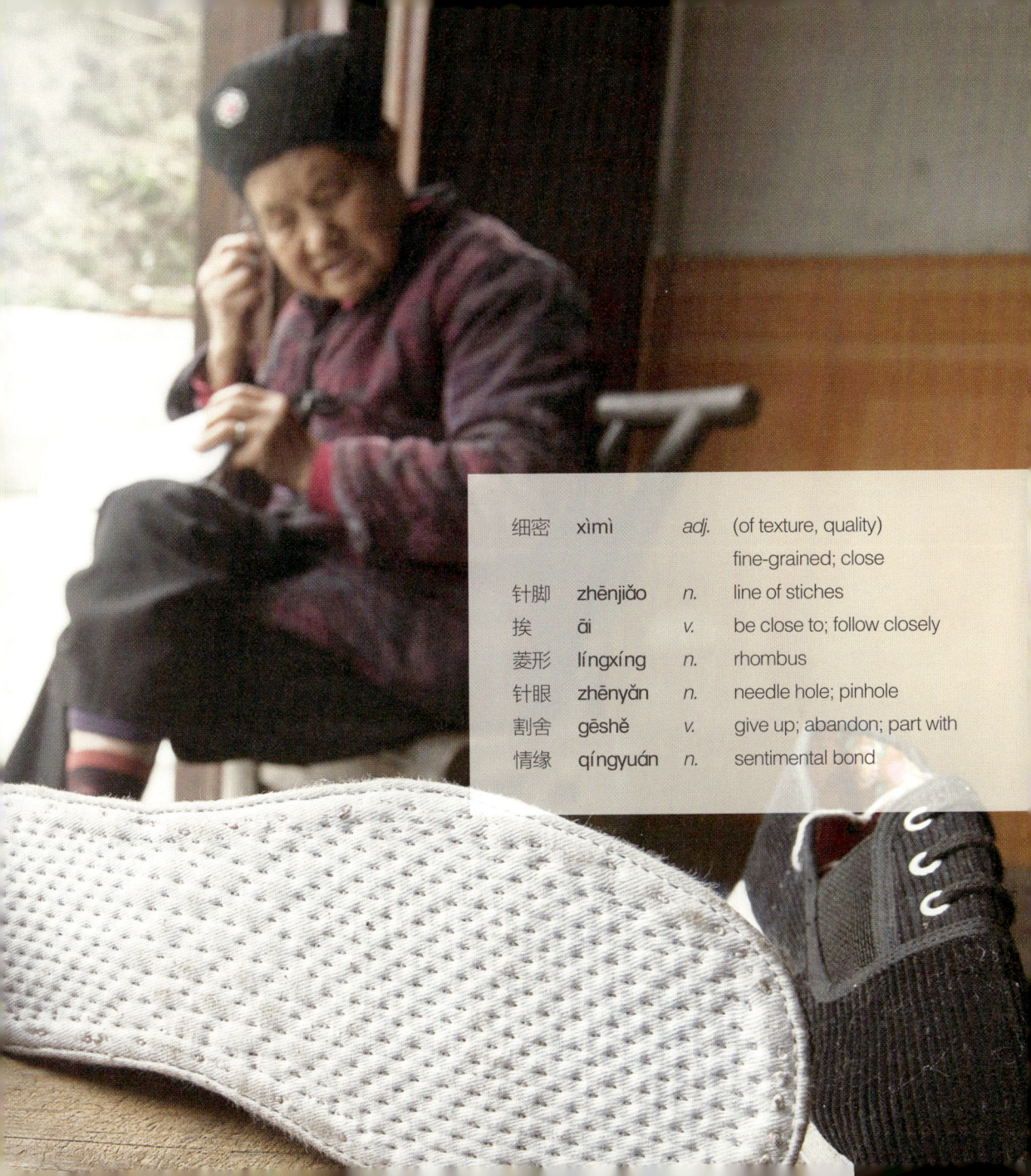

细密	xìmì	adj.	(of texture, quality) fine-grained; close
针脚	zhēnjiǎo	n.	line of stiches
挨	āi	v.	be close to; follow closely
菱形	língxíng	n.	rhombus
针眼	zhēnyǎn	n.	needle hole; pinhole
割舍	gēshě	v.	give up; abandon; part with
情缘	qíngyuán	n.	sentimental bond

延伸阅读 Extensive Reading

中国布鞋的时尚转身
The Fashionable Turn-round of China's Cloth Shoes

中国布鞋有着数千年的历史，以老北京布鞋为代表。创始于1853年的北京内联升是以生产、制作千层底布鞋而闻名的老字号鞋厂，被称为"中国布鞋第一家"。布鞋用料以布料为主，多为平底，鞋底用棉线手工纳制，具有透气、舒适、轻便等特点，深受人们喜爱。

皮鞋生产工艺进入中国以后，由于设计时尚，很快就抢占了老北京布鞋的市场。手工布鞋开始淡出中国人的时尚视野，甚至一度被视为"老土"的象征。于是，以内联升为代表的布鞋企业进行了创新，融合皮鞋工艺和现代设计，突破传统的束缚，实现了古典与时尚的结合。如今，随着种类和款式的丰富与发展，许多追求个性和时尚的年轻人也喜欢上了布鞋。对于传统布鞋的复兴，内联升董事长程来祥认为，布鞋和皮鞋代表着两种文化。皮鞋和西装代表着快节奏的商务化生活方式，而布鞋蕴含着舒适休闲的"家"文化。中式布鞋作为流行时尚再次复苏并不是一种偶然，它反映了人们对精致生活的渴望。

在中国土家族、侗族等民族的风俗中，送布鞋是姑娘传情的一种方式。男女双方的感情如果发展得很好，女方便会给男方送一双手艺精巧的布鞋。结婚时，新郎穿的布鞋做得特别讲究，鞋底一般是白色的，象征高尚纯洁的爱情，而鞋面上的精美花鸟则象征着美满幸福。

2008年，内联升千层底布鞋制作技艺被列入了中国国家级非物质文化遗产名录。手工布鞋正在时尚转身，回归人们的日常生活。

Chinese cloth shoes have a history of thousands of years, with Beijing cloth shoes as the most well-known examples. Founded in 1853, Beijing Neiliansheng Shoe Store is a time-honoured shoe factory famous for producing cloth shoes with multi-layer outsoles. It is reputed as "China's No.1 Cloth Shoe Store". Cloth shoes are mainly cloth-made and flat-heeled. Their outsoles are handmade with cotton threads. Such shoes are breathable, comfortable and lightweight, and therefore are well fond of by people.

Leather shoes soon took over the market of Beijing cloth shoes after entering China because of their fashionable designs. Handmade cloth shoes then began to slide out of Chinese people's view, and were even regarded as an "old-fashioned" symbol for some time. Therefore, cloth shoe factories represented by Neiliansheng made innovative attempts, incorporating the craftsmanship of leather shoes and modern designs, breaking through traditional constrains, and achieved the final combination of classical and fashionable features. Nowadays, as cloth shoes develop more varieties and styles, many young people in pursuit of individuality and fashion have become fond of them. As for the revival of traditional cloth shoes, Cheng Laixiang, the chairman of Neiliansheng, believes that cloth shoes and leather shoes represent two cultures, namely, leather shoes and suits as a symbol of fast-paced, commercialised lifestyle and cloth shoes as the embodiment of the comfortable and leisure culture of "home". The revival of Chinese cloth shoes as a fashion trend is not an accident; it reflects people's desire towards a fine life.

In customs of some ethnic groups such as the Tujia and the Dong, giving cloth shoes as gifts is a way to show the girls' affection. If a romantic relationship goes well, girls will give boys a pair of exquisite handmade cloth shoes. At their weddings, bridegrooms will wear delicate handmade cloth shoes. Generally, the outsoles of the wedding shoes will be white, as a symbol of noble and pure love, and the beautiful flowers and birds on the uppers of shoes represent happiness.

In 2008, the craftsmanship of handmade cloth shoes with multi-layer outsoles of Neiliansheng was included in the List of China's National Intangible Cultural Heritage. Handmade cloth shoes are becoming fashionable again, and are coming back to people's daily life.

 **Cultural Links**

请扫描下方二维码，观看视频《千层底布鞋》，听内联升制鞋师傅讲述千层底的制作工艺和品质。

Please scan the QR code below to watch the video *Cloth Shoes with Multi-layer Outsoles* and listen to the shoe-making master from Neiliansheng talking about the craftsmanship and the quality of such shoes.

Qīxún lǎo piàoyǒu
七旬老票友
A 75-year-old Amateur Beijing Opera Performer

HSK 5级

于兴亭，今年75岁，是一个京剧票友活动站的创始人之一。虽然每次上台演的都是小角色，但他非常开心。

Yu Xingting, 75 years old, is one of the founders of a Beijing opera club for amateur performers. He still enjoys performing despite only playing minor roles on stage each time.

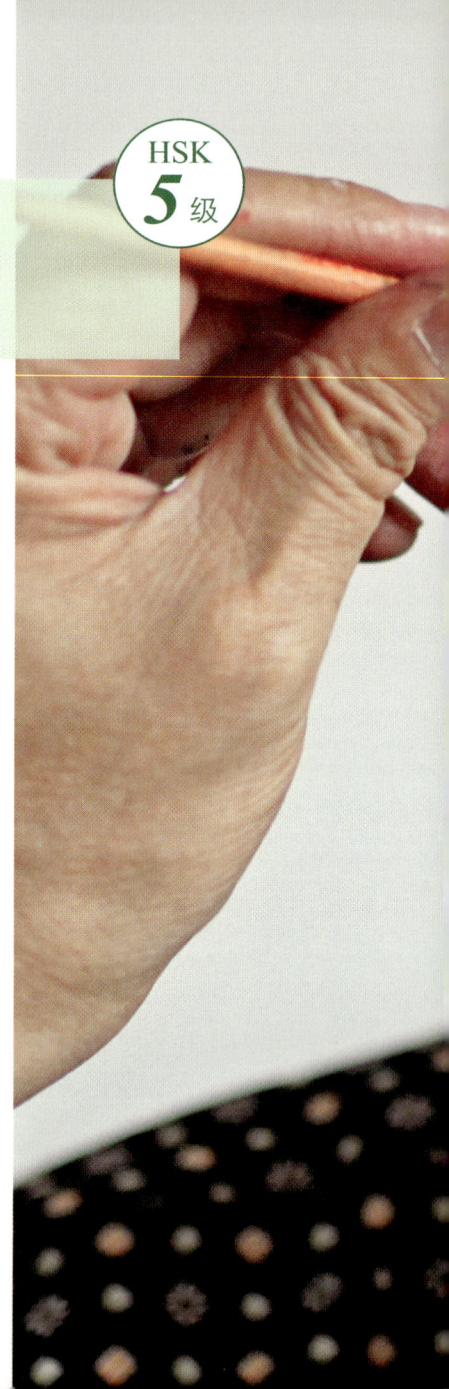

在长春市一个京剧票友活动站内，一位七旬老人正与搭档在舞台上表演武打戏。老人身手敏捷，脚步轻盈，动作让人眼花缭乱。台下观众连连叫好，大呼过瘾。老人名叫于兴亭，今年75岁，是这个京剧票友活动站的创始人之一。

京剧	jīngjù	n.	Beijing opera
票友	piàoyǒu	n.	amateur performer (of Beijing opera, etc)
旬	xún	n.	ten-year period
舞台	wǔtái	n.	stage
武打	wǔdǎ	n.	kung fu fighting
身手	shēnshǒu	n.	dexterity; skill
轻盈	qīngyíng	adj.	slim and graceful
眼花缭乱	yǎnhuā-liáoluàn		be dazed/dazzled
叫好	jiàohǎo	v.	applaud; shout "bravo"
创始人	chuàngshǐrén	n.	founder; initiator

　　于兴亭是长春市自行车厂的退休工人，老家在山东青岛，七岁时跟着父母来到吉林长春。他从小就爱看京剧，尤其痴迷武戏，八岁开始拜师学习，一学就是八年。十七岁的时候，于兴亭在剧场看了一折武戏。戏中人物的高难度动作彻底征服了他。

　　活动日的时候，于兴亭就去活动站排戏、唱戏。一年四季，风雨无阻。

老家	lǎojiā	n.	native place
痴迷	chīmí	v.	be crazy (about/on)
拜师	bàishī	v.	be formally apprenticed to
剧场	jùchǎng	n.	theatre
折	zhé	m.	scene (in a play); act
难度	nándù	n.	degree/level of difficulty
排戏	páixì	v.	rehearse a play/show

● **文化宫** wénhuàgōng
文化宫是一种文化娱乐场所，一般由政府为公众开设，里面设有电影院、图书馆、表演厅、棋牌室、台球房、排练室等。
Cultural palace is a place for cultural activities and entertainment, generally funded by the government and open to the public. A cultural palace usually includes a cinema, library, performance hall, chess and card room, billiard room and rehearsal room, etc.

  1980年4月，长春市文化宫招收京剧学员，于兴亭听到消息后想要试一试。由于他的唱功一般，考试时他就表演了一些武戏动作。因为他的精彩表现，市京剧团录取了他。

于兴亭在与搭档交流。

招收	zhāoshōu	v.	recruit; take in
学员	xuéyuán	n.	student; trainee
唱功	chànggōng	n.	art of singing; singing
团	tuán	n.	group; society

当时文化宫招收学员为的是培养新生力量,于兴亭在学习班里非常刻苦,每天早来晚走,进步很快。他在京剧《法门寺》中饰演一个丑角,300多字的台词能一气呵成地背完。这场戏他两个月演了八场,这次学员班的经历让于兴亭受益匪浅。

新生	xīnshēng	adj.	newly emerging
法门寺	Fǎmén Sì	p.n.	name of a Beijing opera
饰演	shìyǎn	v.	play the role of
一气呵成	yíqì-hēchéng		do sth without interruption
受益匪浅	shòuyì-fěiqiǎn		benefit a great deal (from sth)

于兴亭在排练。

舞台上各种武戏的基本功，为他日后的演出打下了坚实的基础。如今，75岁的于兴亭老人仍然活跃在京剧舞台上。他在票友活动站经常反串饰演花旦等角色。

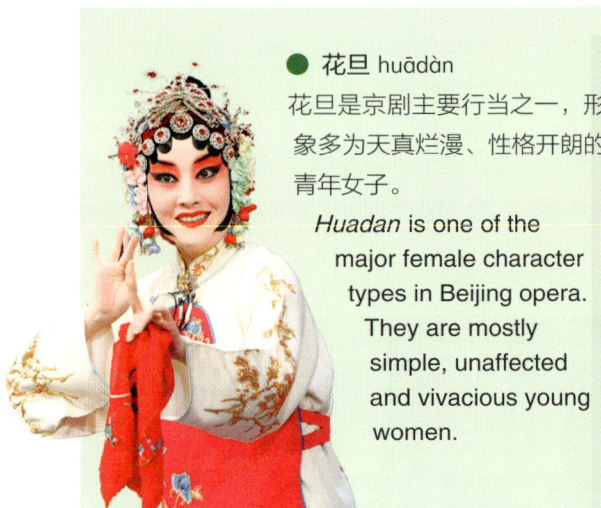

● 花旦 huādàn
花旦是京剧主要行当之一，形象多为天真烂漫、性格开朗的青年女子。

Huadan is one of the major female character types in Beijing opera. They are mostly simple, unaffected and vivacious young women.

基本功	jīběngōng	n.	basic skill; essential technique
日后	rìhòu	n.	future; days to come
坚实	jiānshí	adj.	solid; steady
反串	fǎnchuàn	v.	(in traditional opera) play a reverse role or in a role one is not trained for

于兴亭在表演前化妆。

于兴亭在穿丫环的戏服。

于兴亭化妆后吃了个简单的午饭,准备演出。这次他在京剧中饰演一个丫环的角色。

为了更符合角色的要求,于兴亭还在家自制演出道具。

丫环	yāhuan	n.	servant girl; maid servant
自制	zìzhì	v.	make by oneself
道具	dàojù	n.	stage property; prop

　　平时早上六点，于兴亭就出门遛狗。他养狗已经十年，与爱犬感情很深，每天早上都是小狗叫他起床。

　　遛完狗后，于兴亭就去小公园里晨练，与大家交流。武戏的基本功他每天都要练上两个小时。晨练结束后他会去菜市场买菜，然后回家做饭。

遛狗	liùgǒu	v.	walk a dog
爱犬	àiquǎn	n.	pet dog
晨练	chénliàn	v.	exercise in the morning
菜市场	càishìchǎng	n.	food/grocery market in a town

● 二胡 èrhú
二胡是中国传统民族乐器的一种，有两根弦，声音低沉圆润，是京剧伴奏乐器之一。
Erhu is one of China's traditional musical instruments. It has two strings and a low and mellow tone, and is used as an accompanying instrument in Beijing opera.

业余时间，于兴亭经常去京剧团看戏学习。有时候，他也学学拉二胡。

于兴亭老人的退休生活丰富多彩，用他自己的话说就是"自己找乐儿"，让每一天都充满阳光。如今，75岁的他依然喜欢阅读京剧方面的书籍。他说，京剧是他一生最大的爱好，也是他的精神支柱。唱京剧让他心情愉快，精神矍铄。只要自己还能动，就要一直唱下去，尽管饰演的都是配角，但他一直乐在其中。

（本文选编自http://news.qq.com/original/oneday/2053.html，作者：白石。）

丰富多彩	fēngfù-duōcǎi		rich and colourful
支柱	zhīzhù	n.	pillar; backbone
矍铄	juéshuò	adj.	(of the aged) hale and hearty
配角	pèijué	n.	supporting role
乐在其中	lèzàiqízhōng		find pleasure in

 Extensive Reading

京 剧
Beijing Opera

　　京剧是1800年前后在北京形成的。此后，京剧逐渐成长为中国最有影响力的剧种之一，并被视为中国的国粹。

　　京剧的表演主要有四种艺术手段，分别为唱、念、做、打。唱是指按照一定的曲调演唱；念是指带有音乐性的对话和独白；做是指通过动作和表情进行表演；打是指舞蹈化的武术表演。

　　京剧行当是指剧中演员的角色，主要有生、旦、净、丑四种。生是指男性角色，根据角色年龄和身份的不同，又可以分为不同小类。旦是指女性角色，最著名的旦角演员是20世纪20年代出现的"四大名旦"——梅兰芳、程砚秋、荀慧生和尚小云。

　　净一般是长相或性格比较有特点的男性角色，需要勾画不同的脸谱，所以也叫"花脸"。丑则是幽默机智的角色，他们常会在鼻梁上抹一小块白粉。

　　京剧脸谱与角色性格密切相关，比如红色代表忠诚，白色代表奸诈，黑色代表正直或鲁莽，等等。

　　2010年，京剧被联合国教科文组织列入人类非物质文化遗产代表作名录。近些年，京剧在美国、德国、奥地利等地都上演过，古老的京剧正在焕发新的魅力。

Beijing opera arose in Beijing in around 1800. Since then, it has gradually evolved into one of the most influential operas in China, and is regarded as the quintessence of China.

There are four main skills in a Beijing opera performance, namely singing, recital, acting and acrobatic fighting. Singing is to sing according to certain tunes. Recital refers to musical dialogues or monologues. Acting is to perform through body movements and facial expressions. Acrobatic fighting refers to choreographed martial arts.

Roles in Beijing opera are called *hangdang*, including four major types, namely *sheng*, *dan*, *jing* and *chou*. *Sheng* refers to male roles, and is further divided into several categories according to age and identity differences. *Dan* refers to female roles. The most famous *dan* roles in Beijing opera are the Four Major *Dan* Roles of the 1920s, namely Mei Lanfang, Cheng Yanqiu, Xun Huisheng and Shang Xiaoyun. *Jing* generally refers to male roles with distinguished features or characteristics. Their faces need to be painted differently, thus they are also called *hualian*. *Chou* refers to roles of humour and wit. Performers usually paint a white patch on their nose.

The facial makeup of Beijing opera is closely related to the disposition of the roles. For instance, red stands for loyalty, white for fraudulence, black for integrity or recklessness, etc.

In 2010, Beijing opera was included in the UNESCO's Representative List of the Intangible Cultural Heritage of Humanity. In recent years, Beijing opera has been performed in the US, Germany, Austria and many other places. This ancient form of art is glowing with new charm.

 Cultural Links

一、《说唱脸谱》是一首京剧曲调跟流行音乐相结合的歌曲。请扫描二维码，欣赏这首歌。

The song *Rap of Facial Makeup* combines the features of Beijing opera and pop music. Please scan the QR code to appreciate the song.

二、如今，京剧通过与流行艺术的结合获得了创新性发展。请扫描二维码，欣赏新编京剧《王子复仇记》。

Nowadays, Beijing opera has achieved innovative development through incorporating elements from popular art. Please scan the QR code to appreciate the new Beijing opera *Hamlet*.

正月里的焦家"大趴"

Zhēngyuè li de Jiāo jiā "dàpā"

The Big Party at the Jiaos' in the First Lunar Month

焦氏家族生活在甘肃会宁,祖上曾是清朝官员,如今人才济济。正月里的团聚给这个四世同堂的大家庭带来了欢声笑语。

Living in Huining, Gansu Province, the Jiaos are a big family with lots of talents whose ancestors were officials during the Qing Dynasty. Their reunion in the first lunar month brings cheers and laughter to the big family of four generations.

焦崇伟是焦家的大家长，兄弟姐妹八人，上有耄耋之年的母亲，下有欢聚一堂的儿孙。母亲身体不太好，小孩还在睡觉，所以在这张合影中，只有一半的家族成员。

焦崇伟	Jiāo Chóngwěi	p.n.	name of a person
家长	jiāzhǎng	n.	head of a household
耄耋之年	màodiézhīnián		advanced in age; octogenarian age
欢聚一堂	huānjù-yìtáng		be together on a happy occasion
儿孙	érsūn	n.	children and grandchildren; descendants
家族	jiāzú	n.	clan; family

家人们带着礼物陆续来了。焦崇伟的小孙女三秀穿着新衣服，站在门口张望。

门神、灯笼、窗花都洋溢着春节的欢乐气氛。这扇门的后面正是欢聚一堂的焦家。焦崇伟兄弟姐妹里有五家人基本上都住在一起，正月初二这一天的大团聚是这个大家族几十年来的传统。

孙女	sūnnǚ	n.	granddaughter
张望	zhāngwàng	v.	look around
洋溢	yángyì	v.	be permeated with
春节	Chūnjié	p.n.	Spring Festival
扇	shàn	m.	leaf (for doors, windows, etc)
正月	zhēngyuè	n.	first month of the lunar year
团聚	tuánjù	v.	have a reunion

● 门神 ménshén

门神是守卫门户的神仙，指农历新年贴在门上的一种画类。中国各地（尤其是农村地区）过年有贴门神的风俗，人们相信贴门神可以给全家带来平安和吉祥。

The god of doors guards the doors. It is a painting that people put up on their doors during the lunar New Year. This custom prevails in many places (especially in rural areas) of China. People believe that by putting up paintings of the god of doors, their family can be protected and blessed.

● 窗花 chuānghuā

窗花是指贴在窗户上的剪纸。春节期间，中国各地（尤其是农村地区）常常以贴窗花来装饰环境，营造节日气氛。

Chuanghua is the paper-cutting artwork glued to windows. During the Spring Festival, people of many places (especially rural areas) will glue *chuanghua* to their windows for decoration and to add a holiday touch.

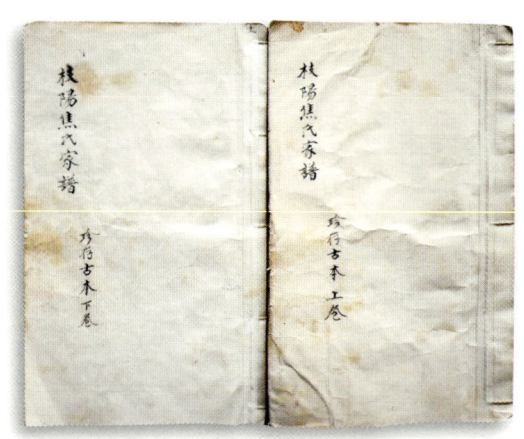

过年期间,焦家有供奉祖先的传统,他们对此十分重视。家谱记录着焦家的家世、家规,维系着家人之间的亲情,见证着家族大团聚的欢乐。

供奉	gòngfèng	v.	make offerings to
重视	zhòngshì	v.	attach importance to
家谱	jiāpǔ	n.	family tree; genealogy
家世	jiāshì	n.	social standing of one's family
家规	jiāguī	n.	family rules
维系	wéixì	v.	hold together; maintain
亲情	qīnqíng	n.	family affection
见证	jiànzhèng	v.	witness

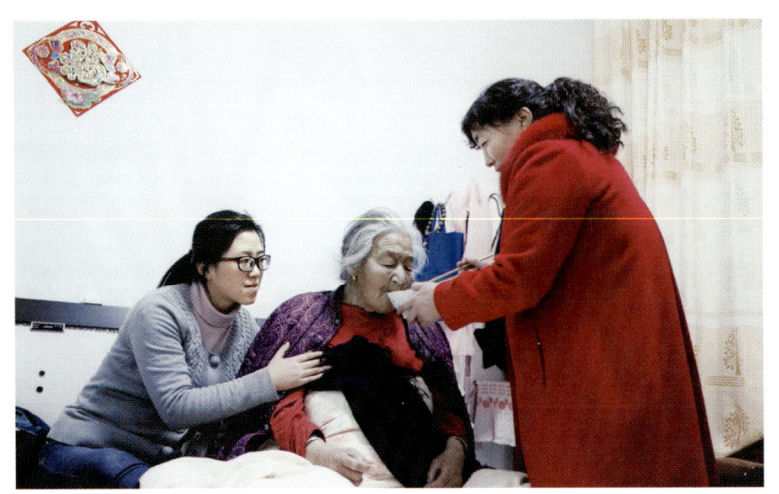

焦家老太太身体不太好，儿孙们就在身边轮流照顾。多在老人身边尽孝，是工作在外的儿孙最大的心愿。

老太太	lǎotàitai	n.	old lady
身边	shēnbiān	n.	one's side
尽孝	jìnxiào	v.	do one's filial duty
心愿	xīnyuàn	n.	wish; dream

祭拜祖先是新春拜年的仪式之一，也是前来拜年的晚辈们表达尊敬的礼数，这在当地很受重视。

祭拜　　jìbài　　　v.　　worship
晚辈　　wǎnbèi　　n.　　younger generation

自然	zìrán	adv.	naturally
大人	dàren	n.	adult; grown-up
供	gōng	v.	supply; provide
就餐	jiùcān	v.	have/take a meal

因为人多,大家吃饭会坐成好几桌。孩子们向来都是坐在一起的,五岁的姐姐会很<u>自然</u>地照顾两岁的弟弟,不需要<u>大人</u>操心。

大锅做饭,饭菜分份。同样的饭菜要装好几个盘子,<u>供</u>大家分桌<u>就餐</u>。

过年时，男人们最开心的是在推杯换盏之间，谈谈国家大事，聊聊家长里短。

孩子们最开心的则是收红包。在焦家，同辈之间有"讨红包"的习俗。晚辈也会给自己的长辈发红包，祝愿他们晚年安康。

推杯换盏	tuībēi-huànzhǎn		toast all around
家长里短	jiācháng-lǐduǎn		domestic trifles/trivialities
同辈	tóngbèi	n.	people of the same generation
讨	tǎo	v.	ask/beg for
晚年	wǎnnián	n.	old age; one's later years
安康	ānkāng	adj.	well and safe

唱歌是必须进行的娱乐项目。从革命歌曲到流行歌曲，从秦腔到神曲，家中老少轮番上阵。

秦腔	qínqiāng	n.	Shaanxi opera (popular in the northwestern provinces of China)
轮番	lúnfān	adv.	by turns; in turn
上阵	shàngzhèn	v.	take part in a match

神曲 shénqǔ
网络语言，指一些旋律简单、节奏鲜明、容易上口、流传较广的歌曲，有时也指一些风格奇异、很难演唱的歌曲。
It is an Internet buzzword that refers to widespread and catchy songs with simple and distinct rhythms. Sometimes it also refers to some bizarre and difficult songs.

孩子们爱跳爱玩。吃过午饭后,他们就在院子里开心地跳起了《小苹果》。

院子	yuànzi	n.	courtyard; compound
小苹果	Xiǎo Píngguǒ	p.n.	name of a popular song

孩子们的拔河比赛，引来了大人们上前助阵，疼爱孙子的爷爷奶奶们也加入了比赛。

大人们也来了兴致，玩起了跳绳。这是他们上学时经常玩的游戏。如今，只有家人们聚在一起时才有这样的兴致。

拔河	**báhé**	v.	tug-of-war
助阵	**zhùzhèn**	v.	boost the morale of; cheer (for)
加入	**jiārù**	v.	join
兴致	**xìngzhì**	n.	interest; mood to enjoy
跳绳	**tiàoshéng**	n.	rope skipping

玩乐之时，大人们即兴表演了社火舞狮。今年，这个家族有数十位成员要参加社火晚会。

玩乐	wánlè	v.	have fun
即兴	jíxìng	v.	improvise
晚会	wǎnhuì	n.	social evening; evening party

● 社火 shèhuǒ

社火是中国民间在节日时举行的大型游艺活动，如舞龙、舞狮等。

Shehuo are large-scale folk festivities held on Chinese festivals, including dragon dance, lion dance, etc.

● 舞狮 wǔshī

舞狮是中国的一种民间艺术，重大节日或集会常以舞狮来庆祝。每头狮子一般由两个人合作表演，一人舞头，一人舞尾，装扮成狮子的样子，做出狮子的各种形态动作。

Lion dance is a form of folk art in China. It is usually performed during festivals or on important occasions for celebration. A lion is usually operated by two dancers, with one dancing as the lion head and the other as the tail. They mimic a lion's movements in a lion costume.

作为父母，最开心的事就是家人们能够聚在一起，让孩子们在 和和美美 的家庭环境中快乐成长。

作为孩子，他们在相互关爱中，不知不觉地延续着家族的这一份亲情与温暖。

和和美美	héhéměiměi		harmonious and happy
相互	xiānghù	adv.	mutually; reciprocally
关爱	guān'ài	v.	show solicitude for
不知不觉	bùzhī-bùjué		unconsciously; unknowingly

这是焦崇伟一家人24年前的照片，那时的焦崇伟风华正茂。

风华正茂　　**fēnghuá-zhèngmào**　　in one's prime

24年后，已是爷爷的焦崇伟儿孙满堂，享受着他们陪伴的幸福。

| 儿孙满堂 | érsūn-mǎntáng | | have children and grandchildren in the household |
| 陪伴 | péibàn | v. | accompany |

这里是焦家原来生活的地方，如今都是在建的高楼。焦家人搬离了祖辈们生活的土地，但仍保留着乡村大院的生活方式和家族父老之间的亲情人情。

（本文选编自http://news.qq.com/original/oneday/1886.html，作者：郝文辉。）

祖辈	zǔbèi	n.	ancestors; ancestry
乡村	xiāngcūn	n.	village; countryside
父老	fùlǎo	n.	elders

 Extensive Reading

中国的家庭
The Chinese Family

每个家庭虽小,却是社会的重要组成部分。伴随着中国社会已经或正在发生的深刻变革,中国的家庭结构也在发生着变化。

祖孙四代人生活在一起的四世同堂曾经是中国最普遍的传统家庭结构,这是因为中国人非常重视家庭和血缘关系,也讲究"养儿防老",家庭观念很强。在生产力较低的年代,大家庭的成员们住在一起,也便于相互帮助,相互支持。进入现代化社会后,人们的生活水平大幅提高,家庭观念也发生了较大的改变,传统的四世同堂大家庭逐渐瓦解。

中国一直都是人口大国。人口基数大、增长过快带来了居住条件差、就业困难、资源短缺等问题。因此,中国逐步将计划生育政策定为基本国策[1]。中国由此出现了很多三口之家,即父亲、母亲和一个孩子组成的家庭。计划生育政策有效地控制了人口增长速度,但人口老龄化、性别比例失衡、劳动力短缺、独生子女压力大等问题也随之而来。

为解决这一困境,计划生育政策逐渐放开,新政策相继出台。从2016年1月1日起,所有夫妇都可以生育两个孩子,部分中国家庭由三口之家变成了四口之家。此外,近些年来,一个人的单人家庭、只有夫妻的丁克家庭以及老人独居的空巢家庭等家庭模式也不断涌现。

现在,二人家庭、三人家庭是主体,由两代人组成的核心家庭占六成以上。从四世同堂到三口之家,再到四口之家、丁克家庭、单人家庭,中国的家庭规模在小型化,类型则在多样化。

---

[1] 计划生育政策详情可参考《中国人的生活故事(第二辑)三十而立》之"家里多了个妹妹"。

Each family, although small, is an important part of society as a whole. With the profound changes that Chinese society has been undergoing, Chinese family structure is also changing.

A family of four generations with great-grandparents and great-grandchildren living together was the most common Chinese family structure. This is because Chinese people attach great importance to family and kinship, and they also believe that children are raised to support parents in their later years. So there is a strong sense of the value of family among Chinese people. In years of low productivity, it was convenient for members of the family living together to help and support each other. However, in today's modern society, people's living standards have greatly improved, and the concept of family has changed a lot. The traditional four-generation family has gradually collapsed.

China has always been a populous country. Its large population base and rapid population growth brought problems such as poor living conditions, unemployment issues and a shortage of resources. Thus, China made family planning policy a basic state policy step by step. As a result, many "families of three" came into being, namely families consisting of a father, a mother and a child. The family planning policy effectively controlled population growth, yet brought about problems such as an aging population, imbalanced sex ratio, labour shortages, and increased pressure on the only child, etc.

To help solve this dilemma, family planning policy has been loosened up and new policies introduced. From 1 January, 2016, all couples in China are allowed to have two children. As a result, some Chinese families went from a "family of three" to a "family of four". In addition, in recent years, new family

patterns are emerging, such as one person living alone, DINK couples without children, and "empty nest" families consisting of only elderly people.

Nowadays, the family of two or three is the mainstream family pattern, and nuclear families consisting of two generations account for over 60% of Chinese families. From "four-generation family" to "family of three", and then "family of four", DINK family, single-person family, the Chinese family is getting smaller in size and more diversified in structure.

 **Cultural Links**

一、汉语中有很多关于"家"的民谚，可以反映中国人的家庭观念，试着了解一下吧。

There are many folk proverbs about family in Chinese, and they represent the family values of Chinese people. Try to learn some of those proverbs.

例如：家和万事兴。
Jiā hé wàn shì xīng.

Harmony in the family leads to prosperity in all undertakings.

二、中国人的亲属称呼条理分明，尊卑有序。请扫描二维码，听一听《辈分歌》，看看在传统中国大家庭中应该怎么称呼长辈们。

The Chinese have a very clear system to call their relatives, which implies hierarchy and order in the family. Please scan the QR code to listen to the *Kinship Song*, and learn how to address the elders in a traditional Chinese family.

Gǔchéng "lǎowántóng"
古城"老顽童"
The "Kidult" in an Ancient Town

HSK 6级

李庆元老先生今年75岁了。他每天和朋友们一起吹拉弹唱，还自学了摄影和电脑后期制作，大家都叫他"老顽童"。

Mr Li Qingyuan is 75 years old this year. He spends his days playing the musical instruments and singing songs with friends. He has also learned photography and postproduction by himself, and is nicknamed the "kidult".

● **文工团** wéngōngtuán
文工团是用唱歌、跳舞等多种形式开展宣传活动的文艺团体。
An art troupe is an art group which launches publicity campaigns through singing, dancing and other art forms.

● **三弦** sānxián
中国传统弹拨乐器，因为有三根弦而得名，是艺人说书时的主要乐器。
Sanxian, a traditional Chinese plucked string instrument, is named after the three strings it has. It is a major accompanying instrument for a storytelling artist.

75岁的李庆元老先生现在比上班族还忙。半个多世纪前他是部队文工团弹三弦的文艺兵，现在他是活跃在山东省青州市古城里的一位"老顽童"。他说累了大半辈子，人到夕阳突然"活明白了"，余生要玩得充实，玩得快乐，玩得有意义。

上班族	shàngbānzú	n.	office worker
部队	bùduì	n.	army
弹	tán	v.	play
老顽童	lǎowántóng	n.	kidult
夕阳	xīyáng	n.	final stage of a person's life
余生	yúshēng	n.	rest of one's life

早晨六点,李庆元准时起床,一番洗漱之后,他开始了每天的"早课":穿上大褂,对着镜子练习说相声。他希望曾经的文艺底子能给自己增加几分自信。

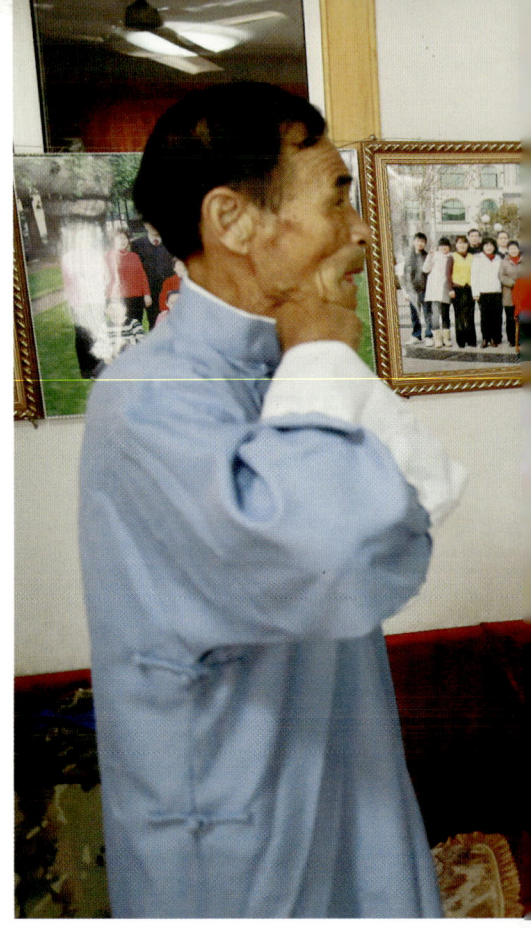

洗漱	xǐshù	v.	wash one's face and rinse one's mouth
早课	zǎokè	n.	(of Buddhist monks) chanting of sutra early in the morning
相声	xiàngsheng	n.	crosstalk
底子	dǐzi	n.	foundation; groundwork

● 大褂 dàguà

大褂是一种长度超过膝盖的中式单衣。中国的相声演员一般穿大褂表演。

A Chinese long gown is an unlined garment which is long enough to cover one's knees. China's crosstalk performers usually wear such long robes on stage.

● 弹拨乐器 tán-bō yuèqì
弹拨乐器是用手指或拨子拨弦的乐器的总称，如三弦等。
The plucked string instrument is the generic term for musical instruments which are played by plucking the strings with the fingernails or plectrums, such as the *sanxian*.

● 弓弦乐器 gōng-xián yuèqì
弓弦乐器是由弓与弦组成的乐器，演奏方式是用弓摩擦琴弦，如二胡等。
A bowed string instrument consists of bows and strings. It is played by a bow rubbing the strings, such as the *erhu*.

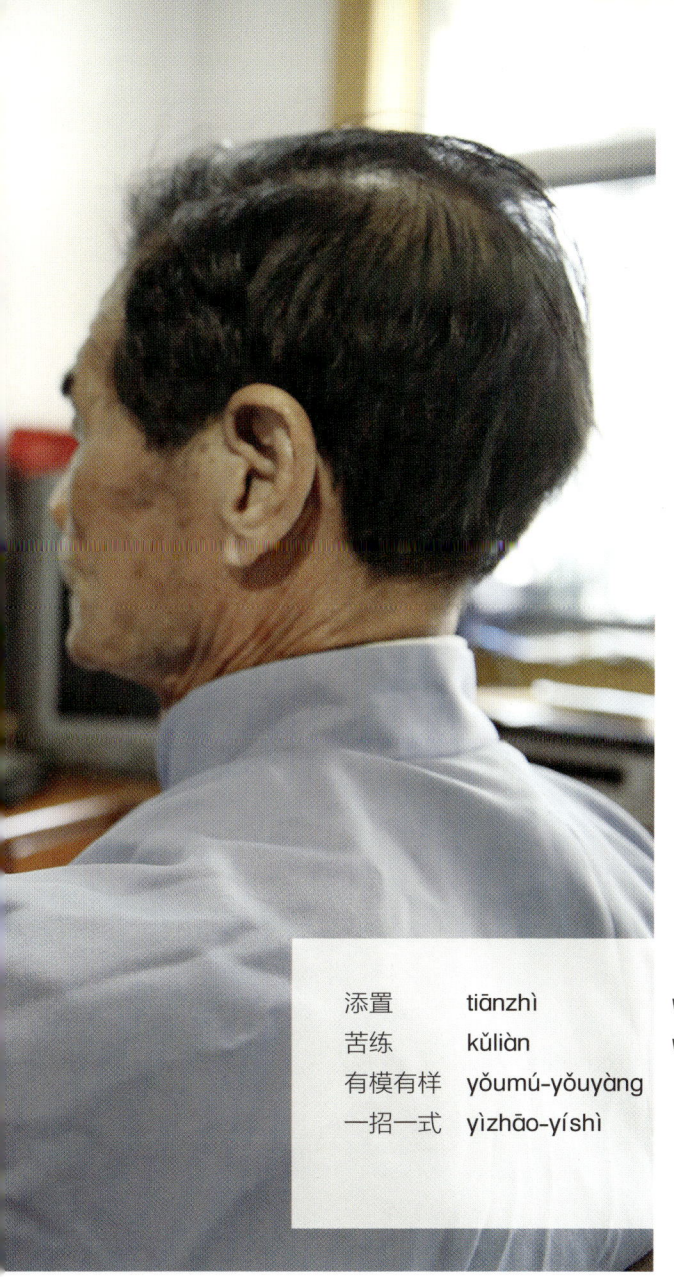

李庆元年轻时当文艺兵学的是弹拨乐器，主要是三弦。去年，他又悄悄添置了二胡等弓弦乐器。经过大半年每天早上一小时的苦练，李庆元现在已经拉得有模有样了，他说："不仅仅是声音，我得练得一招一式都接近专业。"

添置	tiānzhì	v.	add to one's possessions
苦练	kǔliàn	v.	practise hard
有模有样	yǒumú-yǒuyàng		presentable; decent
一招一式	yìzhāo-yíshì		movement and posture in *wushu* or traditional opera

老伴儿跟儿子住在农村,平时李庆元一个人住在城里。当年部队生活给了他超强的生活能力,他活得自由自在、有滋有味。这是他每天的早餐:一只海参、三个从山里买来的鸡蛋、一个馒头、半个猪蹄,还有儿女们送来的新鲜螃蟹。

自由自在	zìyóu-zìzài		leisurely and carefree; free and unrestrained
有滋有味	yǒuzī-yǒuwèi		with enjoyment
海参	hǎishēn	n.	holothurian
猪蹄	zhūtí	n.	pig's foot; trotter
螃蟹	pángxiè	n.	crab

八点半，李庆元骑自行车去"上班"。从家到他"上班"的明清古街骑车只要15分钟。没人想到，这个虎虎生风的老先生早已年过古稀，快奔八十了。

明	Míng	p.n.	Ming Dynasty (1368~1644)
清	Qīng	p.n.	Qing Dynasty (1644~1911)
古街	gǔjiē	n.	ancient street
虎虎生风	hǔhǔ-shēngfēng		vigorous like tigers
古稀	gǔxī	n.	seventy years of age
奔	bèn	v.	(of one's age) get on for; approach

● 捏面人儿 niē miànrénr

捏面人儿是一种中国传统民间艺术。艺人用手和小竹刀通过切、捏、搓等将各种颜色的面团做成一个个生动的作品。

Dough figurine moulding is a form of traditional folk art in China. Craftsmen mould lifelike creatures out of dough of different colours after cutting, pinching and twisting with hands and little bamboo knives.

　　为了营造古街气氛，当地从民间请来几十位艺人，每天上午、下午各两个小时在此进行捏面人儿、唱戏等表演。李庆元就是其中年龄最大的一位。

　　他每天在这条古街上呆四个多小时，与伙伴们一起吹拉弹唱。对于这位"老顽童"来说，这不是一份工作，而是一种玩法，一种生活方式。

营造	yíngzào	v.	create; build
艺人	yìrén	n.	actor; artist
吹拉弹唱	chuī-lā-tán-chàng		blow, pull, pluck and sing—be musically versatile

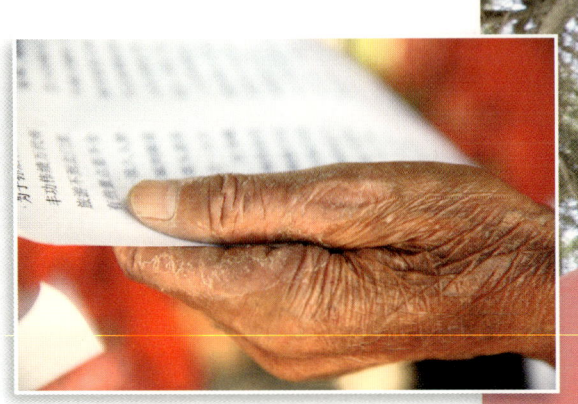

李庆元当过教师，平时喜欢写点儿东西。说唱组的五个成员前几天请他帮着写段**快板书**，他花了几个晚上创作出长达几百句的《山里大嫂逛古城》，获得了大家的一致好评。

创作	chuàngzuò	v.	write; create; produce
一致	yízhì	adj.	identical
好评	hǎopíng	n.	favourable comment

● 快板书 kuàibǎnshū

快板书是一种中国汉族戏曲剧种。表演时，演员一边用两块大竹板和五块小竹板击打节拍，一边说唱。

Rhythmic storytelling is a type of opera performed by China's Han ethnic group. During the performance, the performer recites and sings to the rhythms created by striking a pair of bamboo clappers. The larger clapper has two larger bamboo pieces, and the other one has five smaller bamboo pieces.

中午时分，李庆元请几个老伙伴到古街上一家很有名的餐厅"开荤"。他自称比同龄人会生活，舍得花钱。

平时在家吃完饭后，李庆元会休息一个小时。今天享受完鱼锅他没有回家，而是去古街的树阴下与朋友们楚河汉界较量了一番。

开荤	kāihūn	v.	begin or resume a meat diet
自称	zìchēng	v.	claim to be; profess
同龄人	tónglíngrén	n.	peer
舍得	shěde	v.	be willing to part with
树阴	shùyīn	n.	shade of a tree
较量	jiàoliàng	v.	have a contest

● 楚河汉界

chǔhé-hànjiè

楚河汉界是指象棋棋盘中的分界线，文中指代象棋。

The phrase refers to the boundary line on a Chinese chess board. In this article, it means Chinese chess.

喝着大碗儿茶，跟游人聊聊天儿，谈谈古城的今昔，对李庆元来说，也是个乐子。

李庆元很爱"面子"，隔三岔五就要请古街口的剃头匠给刮刮脸，他说必须把自己最精神的一面展示给别人。

大碗儿茶	dàwǎnrchá	n.	tea served in a big cup
游人	yóurén	n.	tourist
今昔	jīnxī	n.	present and past
乐子	lèzi	n.	fun; pleasure
面子	miànzi	n.	face; reputation
隔三岔五	gésān-chàwǔ		often
剃头匠	tìtóujiàng	n.	barber
精神	jīngshen	adj.	vigorous; lively; spirited

李庆元不久前买了一部摄像机，自学拍摄及视频制作技术。他给自己制订了一个年度计划：他要把他跟伙伴们演奏的曲目和家乡的历史文化美景都拍摄、记录下来，制作成电视片，留给后人。

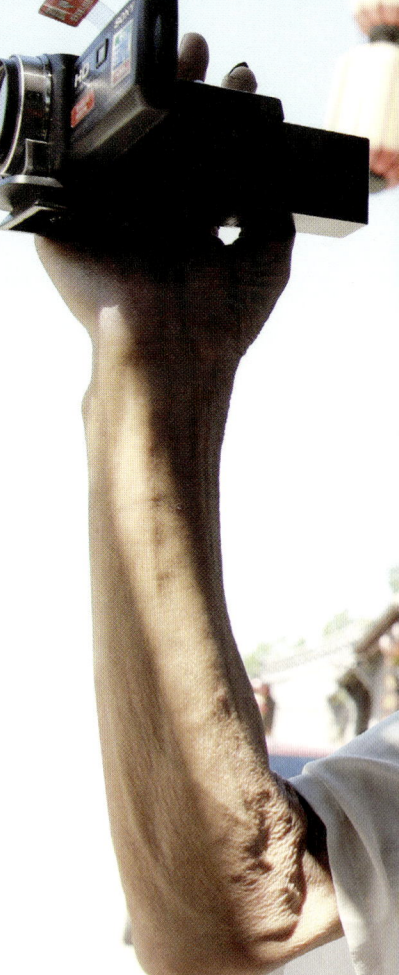

部	bù	m.	(used for machines, vehicles, etc)
摄像机	shèxiàngjī	n.	video camera
自学	zìxué	v.	teach oneself
拍摄	pāishè	v.	shoot
制订	zhìdìng	v.	work/map out
曲目	qǔmù	n.	name of a song, melody or opera
美景	měijǐng	n.	beautiful scenery/landscape
电视片	diànshìpiàn	n.	telefilm; TV film
后人	hòurén	n.	later generation

视频的编辑、制作、配音、加字幕，都是李庆元一个人边学边完成的，虽然慢，但他乐在其中。每次拍摄的内容制作完成后，他都会制作一批光盘，送给被拍摄者和朋友，他说这叫"分享快乐"。一份快乐与大家分享，就成了一片欢乐。

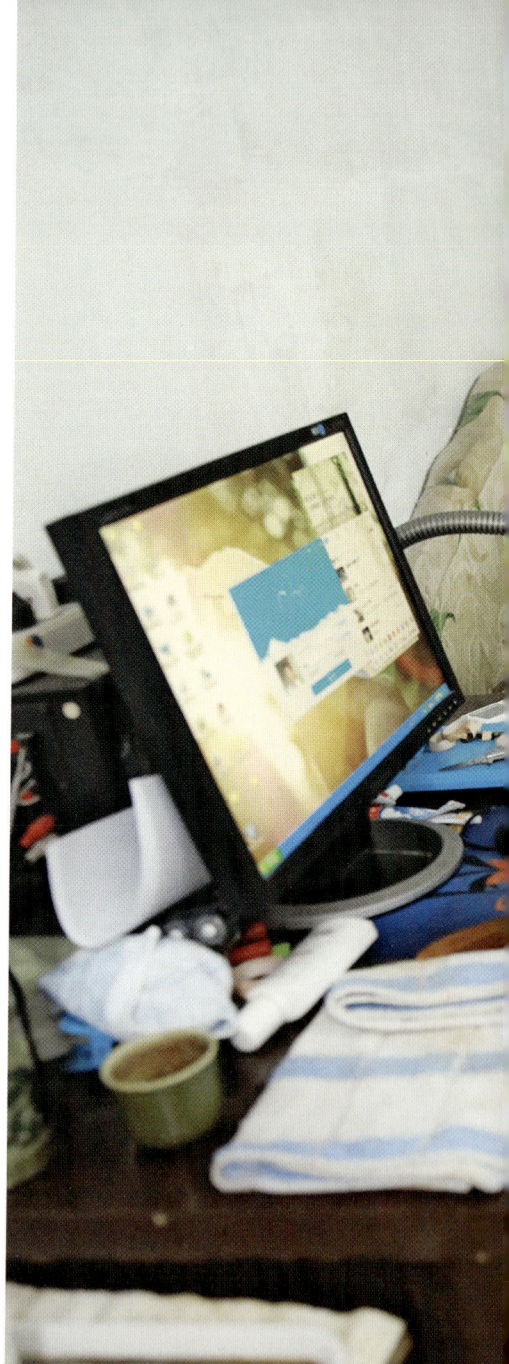

配音　pèiyīn　v.　dub

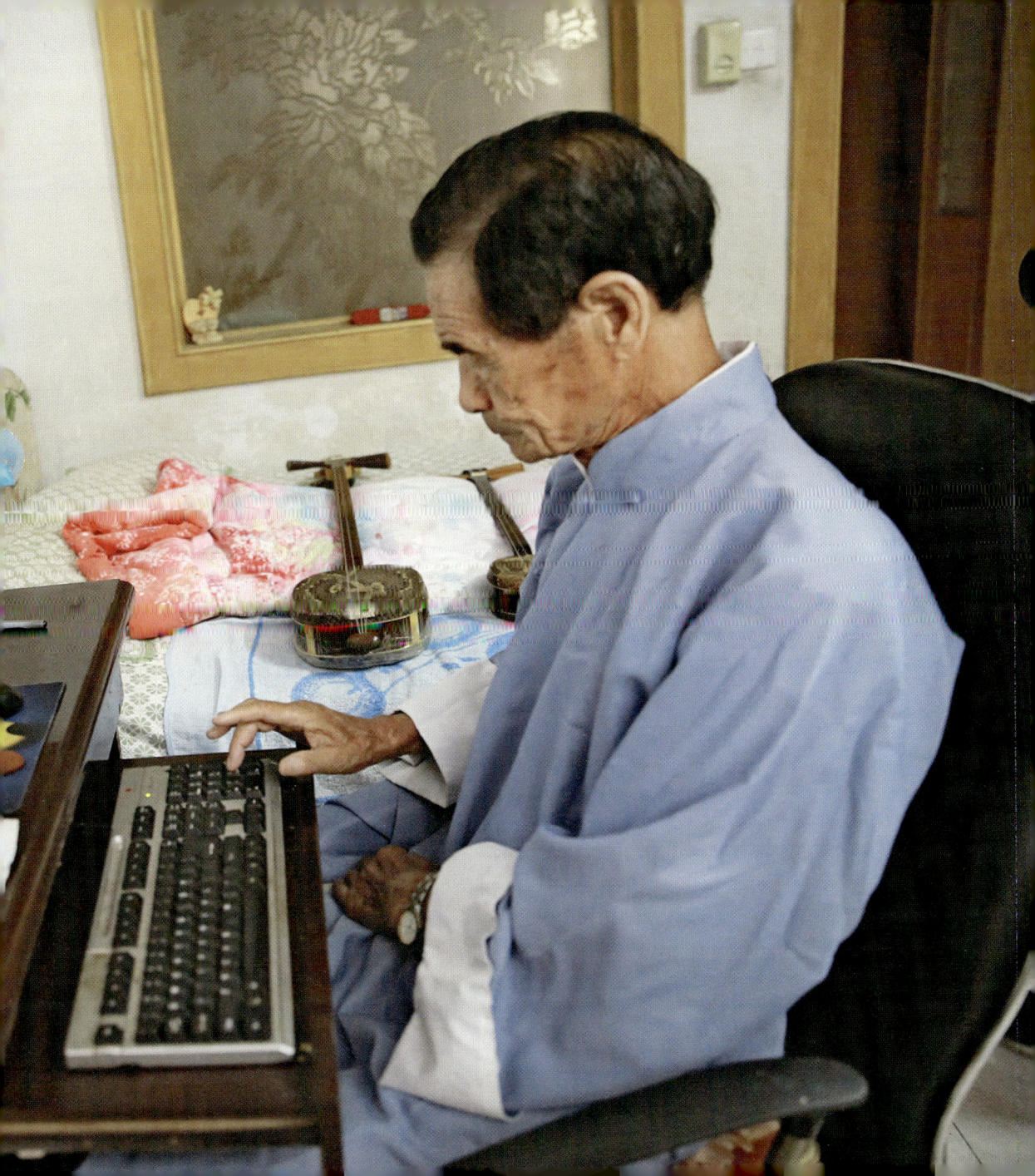

下午"下班"后,李庆元骑车来到南阳河边的城市公园,这里自发形成了多个吹拉弹唱的票友圈子。

晚饭过后,票友们相约在这儿,自拉自唱、自娱自乐。他们会注意控制音量,避免影响市民休息。而不少市民也很认可这种雅致的文化娱乐方式。

(本文选编自 http://news.qq.com/original/oneday/1717.html,作者:施哲莹,施晓亮。)

圈子	quānzi	n.	circle
相约	xiāngyuē	v.	make an appointment
自娱自乐	zìyú-zìlè		amuse oneself
音量	yīnliàng	n.	volume
雅致	yǎzhì	adj.	refined; tasteful

 Extensive Reading

中国民乐
Chinese Folk Music

琵琶

中国传统乐器种类繁多,主要可以分为吹奏类、弓弦类、弹拨类和打击类等四大类。吹奏乐器有笛子等,弓弦乐器有二胡等,弹拨乐器有古筝、琵琶等,打击乐器有锣、鼓等。

中国的少数民族大都能歌善舞,拥有本民族独特的乐器。生长于草原地区的蒙古族喜爱马头琴,这是一种弓弦乐器,琴柱上一般都刻有一个马头作为装饰。哈萨克族的弹拨乐器冬不拉及傣族的吹奏乐器葫芦丝也都是各具特色的民族乐器。

中国民族音乐是指用中国传统乐器以独奏、合奏等形式演奏的音乐。中国民族音乐具有浓厚的民族特色,这主要来源于中国乐器所具有的独特音色及演奏风格。

千百年来,中国音乐家创作了许多优秀的民族音乐曲目,如笛子曲《鹧鸪飞》、二胡曲《二泉映月》、古筝曲《渔舟唱晚》、琵琶曲《十面埋伏》、合奏曲《春江花月夜》等。

中国民乐都比较追求意境，听众在欣赏时常常可以感受到乐曲所表达的各种场景。

很多中国人表示，对当今快节奏的现代都市生活来说，欣赏民族音乐是一种享受，能让人领略到自然质朴的美，唤回内心的平静。

China has a variety of traditional musical instruments, which can be divided into four types, namely wind instruments such as flute, bowed string instruments such as *erhu*, plucked string instruments such as *guzheng* and *pipa*, and percussion instruments such as gong and drum.

China's ethnic minorities are mostly good at singing and dancing, and have their unique musical instruments. Growing up in the prairie region, the Mongolians love *matouqin* (horse-headed *qin*), a bowed string instrument with the top of its neck carved into the shape of a horse's head. The plucked string instrument tambura of the Kazakh ethnic group and the wind instrument *hulusi* of the Dai ethnic group are all distinctive instruments of different ethnic groups.

Chinese folk music refers to the music played by traditional Chinese musical instruments in solo or ensemble ways. Chinese folk music has strong ethnic features, mainly due to the unique tone and performance style of the musical instruments.

For hundreds of thousands of years, Chinese musicians have created many pieces of

古筝

outstanding folk music, such as *The Flying Partridge*, the flute solo, *The Moon Reflected on the Second Spring*, the *erhu* solo, *Singing on Fishing Boats at Dusk*, the *guzheng* solo, *The Ambush on All Sides*, the *pipa* solo, and *A Moonlit Night on the Spring River*, an ensemble.

Chinese folk music focuses on the pursuit of artistic conception. The audience can visualise different scenarios while listening to the music.

Many Chinese people say that the fast-paced, modern city life makes it a treat to enjoy folk music, as it helps people appreciate pristine, natural beauty and recall inner peace.

马头琴

 Cultural Links

一、相声是中国传统说唱艺术。请扫描下方二维码，欣赏相声《戏剧与方言》。

Crosstalk is a form of traditional Chinese storytelling art combing talking and singing. Please scan the QR code below to appreciate the crosstalk *Dramas and Dialects*.

二、请扫描下方二维码，欣赏中国民族乐器合奏曲《春江花月夜》。

Please scan the QR code below to listen to the song *A Moonlit Night on the Spring River*, an ensemble of Chinese folk musical instruments.

词汇索引

词语	拼音	词性	含义	页码
A 挨	āi	v.	be close to; follow closely	63
爱犬	àiquǎn	n.	pet dog	83
安康	ānkāng	adj.	well and safe	105
B 八哥	bāge	n.	mynah	36
拔河	báhé	v.	tug-of-war	109
拜师	bàishī	v.	be formally apprenticed to	73
奔波	bēnbō	v.	rush/dash about	2
奔	bèn	v.	(of one's age) get on for; approach	133
必不可少	bìbùkěshǎo		essential; indispensable	52
标志	biāozhì	n.	sign; mark	28
标注	biāozhù	v.	mark	55
不折不扣	bùzhé-búkòu		downright; sheer	2
不知不觉	bùzhī-bùjué		unconsciously; unknowingly	113
布鞋	bùxié	n.	cloth shoe	48
部	bù	m.	(used for machines, vehicles, etc)	142
部队	bùduì	n.	army	125
C 菜市场	càishìchǎng	n.	food/grocery market in a town	83
唱功	chànggōng	n.	art of singing; singing	75
晨练	chénliàn	v.	exercise in the morning	83
痴迷	chīmí	v.	be crazy (about/on)	73
尺码	chǐmǎ	n.	size	55
出名	chūmíng	v.	gain repute; be famous	26
出身	chūshēn	n.	one's previous experience or occupation	7

词语	拼音	词性	含义	页码
传承	chuánchéng	v.	impart and inherit	48
创始人	chuàngshǐrén	n.	founder; initiator	71
创作	chuàngzuò	v.	write; create; produce	136
吹拉弹唱	chuī-lā-tán-chàng		blow, pull, pluck and sing—be musically versatile	135
春节	Chūnjié	p.n.	Spring Festival	97
从心所欲	cóngxīnsuǒyù		do as one pleases; follow one's inclinations	40
大人	dàrén	n.	adult; grown up	101
大碗儿茶	dàwǎnrchá	n.	tea served in a big cup	141
档案	dàng'àn	n.	file; archive; record	2
道	dào	m.	(for stages in a procedure)	56
道具	dàojù	n.	stage property; prop	81
底子	dǐzi	n.	foundation; groundwork	126
点点滴滴	diǎndiǎndīdī		bit	2
电视片	diànshìpiàn	n.	telefilm; TV film	142
顶针	dǐngzhen	n.	thimble	55
对视	duìshì	v.	look at each other	8
儿孙	érsūn	n.	children and grandchildren; descendants	94
儿孙满堂	érsūn-mǎntáng		have children and grandchildren in the household	115
法门寺	Fǎmén Sì	p.n.	name of a Beijing opera	77
繁琐	fánsuǒ	adj.	complicated and overloaded	60
反串	fǎnchuàn	v.	(in traditional opera) play a reverse role or in a role one is not trained for	78
费事	fèishì	v.	take a lot of trouble	56

词语	拼音	词性	含义	页码
丰富多彩	fēngfù-duōcǎi		rich and colourful	86
风华正茂	fēnghuá-zhèngmào		in one's prime	114
风雨无阻	fēngyǔ-wúzǔ		stopped neither by wind nor rain—regardless of wind and rain	10
父老	fùlǎo	n.	elders	116
副	fù	m.	(for a set of things, etc)	30
G 割舍	gēshě	v.	give up; abandon; part with	63
隔三岔五	gésān-chàwǔ		often	141
工序	gōngxù	n.	working procedure; process	56
供	gōng	v.	supply; provide	102
供奉	gòngfèng	v.	make offerings to	98
购买	gòumǎi	v.	buy; purchase	10
古街	gǔjiē	n.	ancient street	133
古稀	gǔxī	n.	seventy years of age	133
关爱	guān'ài	v.	show solicitude for	113
灌	guàn	v.	fill; pour	15
归功	guīgōng	v.	give credit to	30
H 海参	hǎishēn	n.	holothurian	130
好评	hǎopíng	n.	favourable comment	136
和和美美	héhéměiměi		harmonious and happy	113
后人	hòurén	n.	later generation	142
厚度	hòudù	n.	thickness	55
胡子	húzi	n.	beard; moustache	28

词语	拼音	词性	含义	页码
虎虎生风	hǔhǔ-shēngfēng		vigorous like tigers	133
怀旧	huáijiù	v.	be nostalgic	59
欢聚一堂	huānjù-yìtáng		be together on a happy occasion	94
活儿	huór	n.	work; job	52
货真价实	huòzhēn-jiàshí		out-and-out	25
J 基本功	jīběngōng	n.	basic skill; essential technique	78
即兴	jíxìng	v.	improvise	110
祭拜	jìbài	v.	worship	101
加入	jiārù	v.	join	109
家长里短	jiācháng-lǐduǎn		domestic trifles/trivialities	105
家规	jiāguī	n.	family rules	98
家谱	jiāpǔ	n.	family tree; genealogy	98
家世	jiāshì	n.	social standing of one's family	98
家长	jiāzhǎng	n.	head of a household	94
家族	jiāzú	n.	clan; family	94
坚实	jiānshí	adj.	solid; steady	78
坚守	jiānshǒu	v.	stick to	28
见证	jiànzhèng	v.	witness	98
间隙	jiànxì	n.	gap; interval	34
渐渐	jiànjiàn	adv.	gradually	28
糨糊	jiànghu	n.	paste	51
焦崇伟	Jiāo Chóngwěi	p.n.	name of a person	94
叫好	jiàohǎo	v.	applaud; shout "bravo"	71
较量	jiàoliàng	v.	have a contest	139

词语	拼音	词性	含义	页码
今昔	jīnxī	n.	present and past	141
尽孝	jìnxiào	v.	do one's filial duty	100
京剧	jīngjù	n.	Beijing opera	71
精神	jīngshen	adj.	vigorous; lively; spirited	141
警觉	jǐngjué	adj.	alert	8
镜头	jìngtóu	n.	camera lens	8
就餐	jiùcān	v.	have/take a meal	102
举重	jǔzhòng	n.	weightlifting	33
剧场	jùchǎng	n.	theatre	73
矍铄	juéshuò	adj.	(of the aged) hale and hearty	86
K 开荤	kāihūn	v.	begin or resume a meat diet	139
可谓	kěwèi	v.	it may/can be called	7
苦练	kǔliàn	v.	practise hard	129
矿泉水	kuàngquánshuǐ	n.	mineral water	15
L 老伴儿	lǎobànr	n.	(of old couple) husband or wife	5
老家	lǎojiā	n.	native place	73
老太太	lǎotàitai	n.	old lady	100
老顽童	lǎowántóng	n.	kidult	125
乐天派	lètiānpài	n.	optimist	34
乐在其中	lèzàiqízhōng		find pleasure in	86
乐子	lèzi	n.	fun; pleasure	141
礼数	lǐshù	n.	courtesy; etiquette	52
亮剑	Liàng Jiàn	p.n.	name of a TV serial	26
晾干	liànggān	v.	dry by airing	51

词语	拼音	词性	含义	页码
了如指掌	liǎorúzhǐzhǎng		know sb/sth like the palm of one's hand—know thoroughly	13
菱形	língxíng	n.	rhombus	63
流浪	liúlàng	v.	roam about; drift around	2
遛狗	liùgǒu	v.	walk a dog	83
轮番	lúnfān	adv.	by turns; in turn	106
M 麻线	máxiàn	n.	flaxen/linen thread	55
满脸	mǎnliǎn	n.	entire face	8
慢工出细活	mangong chu xihuo		slow work yields fine products; soft fire makes sweet malt	60
猫粮	māoliáng	n.	cat food	10
猫咪	māomī	n.	cat; kitty	2
毛边	máobiān	n.	(of cloth) rough selvage	55
耄耋之年	màodiézhīnián		advanced in age; octogenarian age	94
美景	měijǐng	n.	beautiful scenery/landscape	142
棉布	miánbù	n.	cotton (cloth)	51
面子	miànzi	n.	face; reputation	141
明	Míng	p.n.	Ming Dynasty (1368~1644)	133
慕名	mùmíng	v.	admire a famous person	59
N 拿手	náshǒu	adj.	good/expert at	33
纳	nà	v.	sew close stitches (over)	48
难度	nándù	n.	degree/level of difficulty	73
年代	niándài	n.	decade of a century	48
P 拍摄	pāishè	v.	shoot	142

词语	拼音	词性	含义	页码
排戏	páixì	v.	rehearse a play/show	73
螃蟹	pángxiè	n.	crab	130
陪伴	péibàn	v.	accompany	115
佩服	pèifú	v.	admire; have admiration for	33
配	pèi	v.	match	7
配角	pèijué	n.	supporting role	86
配音	pèiyīn	v.	dub	144
票友	piàoyǒu	n.	amateur performer (of Beijing opera, etc)	71
朴素	pǔsù	adj.	(of colour, style, etc) simple; plain	60
期间	qījiān	n.	time; period	13
千层底	qiāncéngdǐ	n.	multi-layer outsole	48
亲朋好友	qīnpéng hǎoyǒu		one's relatives and close friends	52
亲情	qīnqíng	n.	family affection	98
亲手	qīnshǒu	adv.	personally; with one's own hand	52
秦腔	qínqiāng	n.	Shaanxi opera (popular in the northwestern provinces of China)	106
青睐	qīnglài	v.	show appreciation; bestow favour	59
轻盈	qīngyíng	adj.	slim and graceful	71
清	Qīng	p.n.	Qing Dynasty (1644~1911)	133
情趣	qíngqù	n.	interest; taste	36
情有独钟	qíngyǒudúzhōng		show special preference/favour to	5
情缘	qíngyuán	n.	sentimental bond	63
亲家	qìngjia	n.	relatives by marriage	52
曲目	qǔmù	n.	name of a song, melody or opera	142
去世	qùshì	v.	die; pass away	13

词语	拼音	词性	含义	页码
圈子	quānzi	n.	circle	147
全球	quánqiú	n.	whole world; entire globe	40
R 日后	rìhòu	n.	future; days to come	78
如数家珍	rúshǔjiāzhēn		as if enumerating one's family treasures with pleasure—be very familiar with and proud of what one is talking about	51
S 散	sàn	v.	distribute; give out	15
纱线	shāxiàn	n.	yarn	55
山村	shāncūn	n.	mountain village	48
扇	shàn	m.	leaf (for doors, windows, etc)	97
善良	shànliáng	adj.	kind-hearted	8
上班族	shàngbānzú	n.	office worker	125
上门	shàngmén	v.	drop in; visit	59
上阵	shàngzhèn	v.	take part in a match	106
舍得	shěde	v.	be willing to part with	139
社区	shèqū	n.	community	5
摄像机	shèxiàngjī	n.	video camera	142
身板儿	shēnbǎnr	n.	body; physique	30
身边	shēnbiān	n.	one's side	100
身手	shēnshǒu	n.	dexterity; skill	71
时至今日	shízhì-jīnrì		even to this day	26
饰演	shìyǎn	v.	play the role of	77
守孝	shǒuxiào	v.	observe a period of mourning for one's deceased parent	28
受益匪浅	shòuyì-fěiqiǎn		benefit a great deal (from sth)	77

词语	拼音	词性	含义	页码
书房	shūfáng	n.	study	40
梳理	shūlǐ	v.	comb	28
树阴	shùyīn	n.	shade of a tree	139
摔跤	shuāijiāo	n.	wrestling	33
双杠	shuānggàng	n.	parallel bars	25
爽朗	shuǎnglǎng	adj.	hearty; frank and open	34
素色	sùsè	n.	plain colour	60
随身	suíshēn	adj.	have/take/bring sth with oneself	15
碎布	suìbù	n.	cloth waste; rag	51
孙女	sūnnǚ	n.	granddaughter	97
台词	táicí	n.	actor's lines	38
谈及	tánjí	v.	speak about	17
弹	tán	v.	play	125
讨	tǎo	v.	ask/beg for	105
讨教	tǎojiào	v.	ask for advice; consult	59
剃头匠	tìtóujiàng	n.	barber	141
替身	tìshēn	n.	substitute; stand-in	30
天下	tiānxià	n.	land under heaven—the world or the whole country	40
添置	tiānzhì	v.	add to one's possessions	129
跳绳	tiàoshéng	n.	rope skipping	109
同辈	tóngbèi	n.	people of the same generation	105
同龄人	tónglíngrén	n.	peer	139
透气	tòuqì	v.	let in air	59
图文并茂	túwén-bìngmào		(of a book, magazine, etc) be excellent in both pictures/illustrations and texts	7

词语	拼音	词性	含义	页码
团	tuán	n.	group; society	75
团聚	tuánjù	v.	have a reunion	97
推杯换盏	tuībēi-huànzhǎn		toast all around	105
外形	wàixíng	n.	appearance	13
玩乐	wánlè	v.	have fun	110
晚辈	wǎnbèi	n.	younger generation	101
晚会	wǎnhuì	n.	social evening; evening party	110
晚年	wǎnnián	n.	old age; one's later years	105
维系	wéixì	v.	hold together; maintain	98
喂养	wèiyǎng	v.	raise; keep	2
武打	wǔdǎ	n.	kung fu fighting	71
舞台	wǔtái	n.	stage	71
夕阳	xīyáng	n.	final stage of a person's life	125
洗漱	xǐshù	v.	wash one's face and rinse one's mouth	126
细密	xìmì	adj.	(of texture, quality) fine-grained; close	63
闲暇	xiánxiá	n.	leisure; free time	36
线	xiàn	n.	thread; string	48
羡慕	xiànmù	v.	admire; envy	33
乡村	xiāngcūn	n.	village; countryside	116
相互	xiānghù	adv.	mutually; reciprocally	113
相约	xiāngyuē	v.	make an appointment	147
相声	xiàngsheng	n.	crosstalk	126
小苹果	Xiǎo Píngguǒ	p.n.	name of a popular song	107
笑意	xiàoyì	n.	smile	8

词语	拼音	词性	含义	页码
鞋帮	xiébāng	n.	upper (of a shoe)	56
鞋底	xiédǐ	n.	sole	51
鞋样	xiéyàng	n.	shoe pattern	51
心愿	xīnyuàn	n.	wish; dream	100
新婚	xīnhūn	v.	be newly married	52
新生	xīnshēng	adj.	newly emerging	77
新闻联播	Xīnwén Liánbō	p.n.	name of a CCTV daily news programme	40
兴致	xìngzhì	n.	interest; mood to enjoy	109
性情	xìngqíng	n.	disposition; temperament	34
学员	xuéyuán	n.	student; trainee	75
旬	xún	n.	ten-year period	71
Y 丫环	yāhuan	n.	servant girl; maid servant	81
雅致	yǎzhì	adj.	refined; tasteful	147
眼花缭乱	yǎnhuā-liáoluàn		be dazed/dazzled	71
洋溢	yángyì	v.	be permeated with	97
一气呵成	yíqì-hēchéng		do sth without interruption	77
一致	yízhì	adj.	identical	136
一招一式	yìzhāo-yíshì		movement and posture in *wushu* or traditional opera	129
艺人	yìrén	n.	actor; artist	135
音量	yīnliàng	n.	volume	147
印	yìn	v.	print	55
营造	yíngzào	v.	create; build	135
游人	yóurén	n.	tourist	141
游刃有余	yóurèn-yǒuyú		handle a butcher's cleaver skillfully—do a job with skill and ease	33

词语	拼音	词性	含义	页码
有模有样	yǒumú-yǒuyàng		presentable; decent	129
有滋有味	yǒuzī-yǒuwèi		with enjoyment	130
余生	yúshēng	n.	rest of one's life	125
豫剧	yùjù	n.	Henan opera	38
院子	yuànzi	n.	courtyard; compound	107
早课	zǎokè	n.	(of Buddhist monks) chanting of sutra early in the morning	126
栅栏	zhàlan	n.	railings; fence	8
张望	zhāngwàng	v.	look around	97
丈人	zhàngren	n.	wife's father	26
招收	zhāoshōu	v.	recruit; take in	75
照料	zhàoliào	v.	take care of; attend to	5
折	zhé	m.	scene (in a play); act	73
针	zhēn	n.	needle	48
针脚	zhēnjiǎo	n.	line of stiches	63
针眼	zhēnyǎn	n.	needle hole; pinhole	63
珍藏	zhēncáng	v.	treasure	52
正月	zhēngyuè	n.	first month of the lunar year	97
支柱	zhīzhù	n.	pillar; backbone	86
制订	zhìdìng	v.	work/map out	142
重视	zhòngshì	v.	attach importance to	98
周边	zhōubiān	n.	neighbouring area	5
猪蹄	zhūtí	n.	pig's foot; trotter	130

词语	拼音	词性	含义	页码
竹篓	zhúlǒu	n.	bamboo basket/crate	51
主攻	zhǔgōng	v.	specialise (in a subject)	26
主人	zhǔrén	n.	owner; possessor	8
主人公	zhǔréngōng	n.	leading character (in a novel, film, etc)	26
助阵	zhùzhèn	v.	boost the morale of; cheer (for)	109
自称	zìchēng	v.	claim to be; profess	139
自创	zìchuàng	v.	create by oneself	33
自然	zìrán	adv.	naturally	102
自学	zìxué	v.	teach oneself	142
自由自在	zìyóu-zìzài		leisurely and carefree; free and unrestrained	130
自娱自乐	zìyú-zìlè		amuse oneself	147
自制	zìzhì	v.	make by oneself	81
棕榈	zōnglǘ	n.	palm	51
祖辈	zǔbèi	n.	ancestors; ancestry	116

中国人的生活故事

Stories of Chinese People's Lives

  《中国人的生活故事》是专为汉语学习者编写的中文系列读物，按主题分为八个分册。每个分册共收录八篇文章，从名家名篇到普通人手笔，这些选文从各个角度讲述现代中国人生活中的点滴故事。这套读物既可以让读者更加了解中国人和中国社会，也可以作为汉语学习的辅助材料，帮助读者提高中文阅读水平。

Stories of Chinese People's Lives series aims to introduce Chinese people's daily life and their stories to Chinese learners and those who are interested in China, and to help them understand more about China and Chinese people. The first collection is published in pocket size, containing 8 books on the themes as: *Taste of Love*, *Colorful Culture*, *Silent Kinship*, *Stage of Life*, *Scenes in Society*, *Sceneries of the world*, *Poems from the Heart* and *Wisdom of Life*.

购买链接